Philosophy of STEM Education

The Cultural and Social Foundations of Education

The Palgrave Pivot series on the Cultural and Social Foundations of Education seeks to understand educational practices around the world through the interpretive lenses provided by the disciplines of philosophy, history, sociology, politics, and cultural studies. This series focuses on the following major themes: democracy and social justice, ethics, sustainability education, technology, and the imagination. It publishes the best current thinking on those topics, as well as reconsideration of historical figures and major thinkers in education.

Series Editor: **A. G. Rud** is Distinguished Professor in the College of Education of Washington State University, USA

Titles include:

Ted Newell
FIVE PARADIGMS FOR EDUCATION
Foundational Views and Key Issues

Craig A. Cunningham
SYSTEMS THEORY FOR PRAGMATIC SCHOOLING
Toward Principles of Democratic Education

Aaron Stoller
KNOWING AND LEARNING AS CREATIVE ACTION
A Reexamination of the Epistemological Foundations of Education

Sue Ellen Henry
CHILDREN'S BODIES IN SCHOOLS
Corporeal Performances of Social Class

palgrave▸pivot

Philosophy of STEM Education: A Critical Investigation

Nataly Z. Chesky
Assistant Professor, State University of New York, New Paltz, USA

and

Mark R. Wolfmeyer
Assistant Professor, Kutztown University, USA

DOI: 10.1057/9781137535467.0001

PHILOSOPHY OF STEM EDUCATION
Copyright © Nataly Z. Chesky and Mark R. Wolfmeyer, 2015.

All rights reserved.

First published in 2015 by
PALGRAVE MACMILLAN®
in the United States—a division of St. Martin's Press LLC,
175 Fifth Avenue, New York, NY 10010.

Where this book is distributed in the UK, Europe and the rest of the world, this is by Palgrave Macmillan, a division of Macmillan Publishers Limited, registered in England, company number 785998, of Houndmills, Basingstoke, Hampshire RG21 6XS.

Palgrave Macmillan is the global academic imprint of the above companies and has companies and representatives throughout the world.

Palgrave® and Macmillan® are registered trademarks in the United States, the United Kingdom, Europe and other countries.

ISBN: 978-1-137-53547-4   EPUB
ISBN: 978-1-137-53546-7   PDF
ISBN: 978-1-137-53545-0   Hardback

Library of Congress Cataloging-in-Publication Data is available from the Library of Congress.

A catalogue record of the book is available from the British Library.

First edition: 2015

www.palgrave.com/pivot

DOI: 10.1057/9781137535467

To the students we currently teach and to all future teachers of mathematics and science.

Contents

List of Illustrations	vii
Series Editor's Preface	viii
Preface	x
Acknowledgments	xiv
1 Introduction to STEM Education	1
2 STEM's What, Why, and How? Ontology, Axiology, and Epistemology	17
3 Critical Inquiry into STEM Education	44
4 Critical Opportunities in STEM Education	75
5 Concluding Thoughts	90
References	95
Index	104

List of Illustrations

Figures

2.1	Axiology, ontology, and epistemology	19
3.1	Analytic constructs for coding	52
3.2	Comparison of total codes	57
3.3	Comparison of average distribution of codes	57

Tables

3.1	Total coding distribution	56
3.2	Distribution of codes per document	58

Series Editor's Preface

The Palgrave Pivot series on the Cultural and Social Foundations of Education seeks to understand educational practices around the world through the interpretive lenses provided by the disciplines of philosophy, history, sociology, politics, and cultural studies. This series focuses on the following major themes: democracy and social justice, ethics, sustainability education, technology, and the imagination. It publishes the best current thinking on those topics, as well as reconsiderations of historical figures and major thinkers in education.

The cultural and social foundations of education are enjoying a rebirth. While studies of Plato, Pestalozzi, and Dewey or analyzes of the effects of Supreme Court decisions or world economic policies have always been important to understand education, there is increased urgency for such work in today's educational climate. Education is seen in both the developed and developing world as a means to social advancement and improvement of life. More than ever there are questions about what kind of education should be provided and for whom. In addition, information technologies are rapidly transforming teaching and learning, while a political climate in many countries emphasizes market solutions to social problems at the same time that it moves away from democratic forms of schooling.

Out of this rich context, the Cultural and Social Foundations of Education series was established to explore five themes important in schooling in short books by leading and rising scholars. I chose themes that are of perennial importance to the foundations of education, such as democracy and social justice, as well as newer emphases, such as technology and sustainability that scholars are exploring. Democracy and social justice has been a perennial theme in foundations of education, and continues to have greater urgency. This series will feature works that examine worldwide issues related to democracy and social justice, from the effects of wealth and income inequality on schools in developed countries to the spread of democracy and social justice concerns to other countries around the world. Closely related to this is the second theme of ethics: issues of right, wrong, fairness, equity, and equality in schools and educational practices worldwide. Increased attention is being paid to our planet's health, so how we can educate our children to accept and deal with environmental degradation forms the third theme. What it means to educate for a sustainable future is a question that foundation scholars are increasingly addressing. For a fourth theme, the impact of information technology upon education is enormous and not something that should be left just to technical experts in that area. There is a need for scholars in the cultural and social foundations of education to inquire critically about the claims made by technology and to inform us about new developments in this area. Finally, the arts and imagination are all too often pushed to the margins of schooling especially today, and so this topic forms the fifth theme. Scholars of foundations have long championed the importance of this area: in the past century, John Dewey made a compelling argument for the importance of art and the imagination and especially for supporting the arts in educational practice in his late work, *Art as Experience*.

The volumes in the series will be both single authored and edited collections, and serve as accessible resources for those interested in foundational issues in education at all levels, particularly advanced undergraduate and graduate students in education and the social sciences who are being exposed to the latest thinking on issues of perennial importance and relevance to the context and practices of education worldwide.

Series Editor
A. G. Rud

Preface

Hanging on a bulletin board outside the main student center in a community college where one of us used to teach was a large poster titled "STEM Careers—Are you ready?" This 3-ft by 2-ft poster hung ominously over the only exit that students were forced to take to and from their classes. A large Bill Gates pointed an accusatory finger at you, while Einstein gave you a knowing smirk, both seeming to want to share a secret. It made you question your chosen major, your life choices, even your very intellectual ability. It was 2010 and Race to the Top was just about to go in full swing; the discourse of competition was rampant with few voices questioning its claims. Once again, a critical eye fell upon the education system of the self-proclaimed world leader: the United States. Politicians worried if there were enough talented citizens to create new technologies in order to secure the country's spot as the dominant world power. Trans-national corporations and local business leaders wondered if there would be enough college graduates to fill their company's positions. Educators, unfazed by yet another reform act, hoped the spotlight would be turned toward communities most in need of federal and state level support and to the larger socio-economic problems that affect the schools within them.

As former public school mathematics teachers, surely we could not disagree with the claim that STEM subjects were important and ought to be given emphasis. As parents of small children, we would be remiss to not admit that we were concerned with the world our children would inherit and how they could navigate successfully through it. But, as educational researchers and theorists, we could not ignore the glaring contradictions in the discourse and not respond in some way to its claims and objectives. We wondered if the teaching of mathematics and science should be subsumed as merely a utilitarian activity needed for technology and engineering skills that are used to further a nation's economic power. And we did not believe that our children's happiness and success equated to their ability to trump their peers and compete with their neighbors, locally or globally.

Both of us began our education careers as public school mathematics teachers.

Nataly stepped right into the policy firestorm so to speak since her first teaching assignment was teaching mathematics to students who failed the state-mandated standardized tests the year before. The school district in which she worked did not meet "National Youth Advocate Program (NYAP)" according to the first year's implementation of No Child Left Behind (NCLB) Act and was therefore threatened to be closed down by the state if they did not raise their math scores by the following year. It did not seem to matter that the students who failed were first-generation English language learners who have only been in America for a few years, nor did the fact that more than half of the students were living at or below poverty and many more were on free and reduced lunches. Mark's work in urban high school math teaching on both coasts reflects a very similar story.

Now, we are both teacher educators working in higher education institutions, where much of our responsibilities center on preparing future mathematics and science teachers. We grapple every semester wondering what knowledge, skills, experiences, and dispositions are integral for our students, and what must be briefly discussed due to time constraints, state requirements, and other variables beyond our control. Unfortunately, one of those knowledges that oftentimes does not make it past the over-ambitious syllabus is the philosophical investigations of mathematics and science education.

Over the years of teaching, we have made a concerted effort to combat that tendency, creating meaningful assignments that ask our students to engage with the histories of the disciplines and their relation to how our educational system has designated them to be taught. We also attempt to make room for experiences for our students to critique policy about mathematics and science education so that they not only have knowledge about the policies they will one day be responsible to implement, but also gain a "critical consciousness" about educational policy and the way in which it affects teachers, students, communities, and society at large. Thus, the vision for this book evolved out of our experiences preparing pre-service teachers in mathematics and science at the university level. Having ridden the wave of reforms in these fields ourselves in our own previous teaching career, we were forced to once again make sense of another iteration of mathematics and science reforms, aimed directly at US public schools.

However, we would like to be clear on the focus of this book and its inherent limitations. Our objective is to attempt a philosophical investigation into STEM education initiatives and the discourses that surround them. This is a broad undertaking and as such requires us to leave out perhaps more than we include. Primarily, our undertaking was to select three philosophical domains (axiology, epistemology, and ontology) and explore the relevant philosophies of mathematics, science, mathematics education, and science education. We did not, for example, use the broad-based literature on philosophy of education and apply that to the distinct STEM subjects (science, technology, engineering, and mathematics) in particular. We gladly accept this limitation and consider it part of the nature of inquiry itself. Indeed, what we hope to accomplish in this book is to sample philosophical domains of thinking that can help articulate how we may come to think about STEM educational reform discourses, what drawbacks or consequences they may hold, and what potentialities may arise from exposing the philosophical assumptions that lie latent in them.

The book's primary audience is anyone interested in current educational policy. Thus, we anticipate little to no prior philosophy training. We hope that readers of this book gain the knowledge of philosophical theories and method for helping them investigate STEM education policies through a philosophical lens and engage in critical analysis of STEM's discourse. After all, as Badiou reminds us, philosophers and theorists ought to serve as "watchmen" or in other words as public scholars always engaged with the socio-political climate that surrounds them. It is easy to get caught up in our day-to-day lives, our teaching, our families, our research, our personal hopes, and struggles. But, we must remember that we are always forever in this world together, tied in complex professional and personal relationships. Badiou also explains that every universal truth can only materialize within a personal situational context. And so it is for our book, which is grounded in our own struggles and research experience in US education. The United States is not at all alone in its embrace of STEM education, which we contend is the prominent educational discourse worldwide. While we can never be an expert in everything, or know all the details of every political event that has consequences for us, we can be moved and deeply affected by a few of them. At this time in history, we feel that, for educators, educational theorists, and parents and learners everywhere, one such event ought to be STEM education. Certainly, this logic also applies to a philosophical investigation into any educational issue, no matter how seemingly well defined. Our philosophical method will only graze the surface of the domain of philosophy proper; in doing so we will delve into a one particular philosopher's point of view, which offers precise insight into how we may make sense of STEM education reform discourses and attempt to envision future possibilities inherent within them.

Let us begin the investigation together and "wake up" so to speak to understand more deeply what we arguably claim is the most influential, most oppressive, and potentially the most revolutionary educational policy of our time.

Acknowledgments

First and foremost we thank Sarah Nathan and the editorial team at Palgrave Macmillan for their work in getting this to print and their extremely helpful feedback in the early stages. In terms of the contents of this book, we are indebted to several scholars for their contributions including but not limited to Rebecca Goldstein, John Lupinacci, and Paul Ernest. Finally and most importantly, we thank our friends and families for their ongoing support of our writing pursuits. Mark would like to especially thank Ellie, Beatrice, Guy, Beth, David, Paul, and Helen. Nataly would like to thank Marc, Vivian, Naomi, Steve, Yefim, Sofia, Alla, and Lenny.

1
Introduction to STEM Education

Abstract: *We provide a brief review of STEM's history, particularly as it relates to the philosophical mode of inquiry used in the book. The introductions here include discussions of STEM as a whole as well as some examples from among STEM subfields, such as mathematics and science education. Notably absent in this review is the use of philosophical methods, thus justifying our present inquiry. In the final section, we motivate our philosophical inquiry with a review of the little scholarship attending to it, mostly the philosophies of mathematics and science that are just beginning to be applied to education research.*

Keywords: history of education; philosophy of education; STEM education

Chesky, Nataly Z. and Mark R. Wolfmeyer. *Philosophy of STEM Education: A Critical Investigation.* New York: Palgrave Macmillan, 2015. DOI: 10.1057/9781137535467.0006.

Since the beginning of the 21st century, increasing attention has been placed on public education in the United States in the fields of mathematics and science. Most recently, the emphasis has been on the education of mathematics, science, technology, and engineering, termed "STEM." Framed as educational equality initiatives that will help students gain the knowledge they need to compete in the global marketplace, STEM may be the most indicative educational reform discourse of our time and has grown to become one of the primary foci of educational policy, in part due to its easy associations to a wide array of today's industries: from information and communications technology to the medical field, to sustainability innovations. Given such connections, we consider STEM as the logical extension of the economic imperative for education that has gained momentum in the past 30 years.

The primary focus of this book is to shift the attention away from the strictly utilitarian aims, geared to quickly and efficiently meet the STEM initiatives, and to take a step back and ask critical questions about what types of aims the STEM initiatives are asking for, what assumptions do such aims hold, and what possible implications or consequences could such initiatives have on various socio-economic groups, funneled through a public education system that is increasingly being tied to economic, capitalistic incentives and procedures. In order to begin to answer the above questions, we will use a philosophical lens to study STEM policies as a political and social phenomenon.

In this chapter, we introduce the material of the book first by providing a brief review of STEM education's history, particularly as it relates to the philosophical mode of inquiry used in the book. The introductions here include discussions on STEM education as a whole as well as some examples from among STEM subfields, such as mathematics and science education. Next, we review critiques of STEM education policy as they relate to our research questions above. Notably absent among this review is the use of philosophical methods, thus justifying our present inquiry. In the final section, we motivate our philosophical inquiry with a review of the little scholarship attending to it, mostly the philosophy of mathematics and science that are just beginning to be applied to education research. Finally, this chapter includes an outline of the remaining contents of this book.

1.1   What is STEM?

"STEM" began as "SMET," standing for science, mathematics, engineering, and technology. In the 1990s the National Science Foundation (NSF) coined the term in order to emphasize the importance of these four distinct disciplines (Sanders, 2009). The acronym was changed to "STEM" to help promote it, yet there are still a considerable number of Americans that associate STEM with stem cell research (ibid.). This is problematic since parents ought to be made fully aware of the kinds of reforms their children will be affected by. Even many educators are unclear about what STEM education is (Breiner et al., 2012). The National Science Foundation explains that STEM education is about proliferating the importance of these four disciplines in the education community and society at large. The acronym is ambiguous, since educators have also used it to describe the inherent interconnectedness between the four disciplines, as well as create curricula and pedagogy that link them together within one year or classroom. Below are several possible ways to understand the STEM reform initiative:

▶ Science, mathematics, engineering, and technology are fields in which the US needs to produce more highly competent workers in order to compete in the future global marketplace.

▶ Science, mathematics, engineering, and technology are inherently linked and therefore it would be advantageous for the learner to have real-life hands-on projects that explain and utilize the interconnectedness of them.

▶ A high level of understanding of the fields of science, mathematics, technology, and engineering are essential knowledge sources for all future democratic citizens, and especially so for minority and underrepresented groups that may not have had access to this important area of knowledge, and this has hampered not only their ability to find a fulfilling job, but also to function as effective citizens (e.g., to get a loan, to understand the voting process, and to manage their credit and money). (Brown et al., 2011; Bybee, 2010)

Perhaps the argument can be made that the three objectives listed above are one and the same, or at the very least complement each other. These three aims are prevalent in most STEM policy reform documents; not only do these three objectives occur relatively equally in the discourse, they occur simultaneously in any given document. For instance, being a high-functioning democratic citizen may also mean having a fulfilling job. Further, generating citizens that increasingly go into technologically skilled jobs helps the nation compete in economic global market. Additionally, understanding the interconnectedness of science, mathematics, technology, and engineering may improve the teaching and learning of these traditionally difficult subjects and therefore enhance the objective of obtaining a high level of literacy in them, which in turn helps to get a job and be a good citizen.

Generally, the STEM initiatives have two main interconnecting objectives at the macro- and micro-level. At the national macro level, it is centrally important as a pillar for cementing the epistemological and pragmatic advances in technology and engineering that our country needs in order to stay economically competitive on a global level. At the microlevel, the objective is for individual students to have a strong understanding of the interdisciplinary link, objectives, and techniques that categorize STEM curricula, in order for them to become critically literate citizens and procure a financially secure employment in their adult lives (e.g., Brown et al., 2011; Bybee, 2010).

All of this is speculation since there is no way for us to clearly gauge what the motives of policymakers are and exactly how the rhetoric found in policy documents matches the varying axiological objectives of STEM education. As we will explain shortly, axiological objectives are a common starting point for philosophical inquiries into education because they point to inherent values and the general worth an educational system provides to society's variety of constituents. What we would like to stress here is that policy discourse is inherently concerned with axiological objectives; therefore it is logical to assume that axiological objectives would be the most diverse and proliferated in the discourse surrounding STEM. Notwithstanding this tautology, policy documents are more than simply axiological objectives about the purposes of education. Axiological objectives present in policies about STEM interact with the other discourses present in policy documents, such as the epistemological claims that specify what pedagogical practices are best for teaching and learning of, say mathematics and science, and ontological assumptions that hint at how the conception of said subjects fundamentally shapes the way they are thought about and used in education. Indeed, there are several presuppositions internal to these educational objectives, such as what STEM content ought to be used for, how STEM practices and thoughts shape the modern world, and the universal quality of the internal concepts themselves, such as numbers or substances. These concepts can be placed in the philosophical category of ontology, which seeks to understand and ask questions about the basic structure of our world. The conviction underlying this book is that these presuppositions must be rigorously investigated, not only to aid in implementation and conceptualization of sound cogent policy reforms in education, but also in reflecting on the societal implications such reform efforts signify.

Thus, answering just what STEM education is proved to be a difficult task. As outlined above, STEM education communicates a concern with content areas that are interconnected and relate to present and future job conditions. Although the acronym is fairly young, it is important to question STEM education's true age and to consider the historical trajectory in educational policy within which it emerged. Often it is argued that STEM education, or at least its seed, initiated in the 1950s with US reactions to the Soviet launch of Sputnik. In fact, the emphasis on STEM education content took place even earlier. In the 1940s engineer Vannevar Bush believed in STEM education content's promise to solve the world's problems. He wrote official statements to President Eisenhower calling for educational structures to prepare the nation's future scientists, which ultimately led to the creation of the National Science Foundation (Spring, 2010). Besides the important social goals of poverty and environmental issues, also in these initial conversations was national defense, a concern given the recent conclusion of World War II. Ultimately, this concern would take on greater prominence with the launching of Sputnik and the Cold War. In 1958, Congress passed the National Defense Education Act, which had specific emphasis on science, mathematics, and technology education. In particular, President Eisenhower emphasized the promotion of STEM careers and the advancement of STEM teaching (ibid.), without calling it STEM, of course as the acronym had not yet been invented.

Such attention to STEM in the United States thus resulted primarily from militaristic concerns. This attention shifted in the early 1980s, as the Cold War waned and the new concerns over economic dominance by West Germany and Japan emerged. The 1983 publication *A Nation at Risk* points specifically to technological advancement as a key concern for US economic vitality. Since then, STEM conversation has continued to center on workforce training. As an example, Tucker (2012), president of the National Center on Education and the Economy, argues that

STEM is a key component to US economic security. Although he reacts against STEM programs, he argues in favor of more competent STEM teachers for the preparation of a STEM workforce. As for what is argued as STEM's content backbone, Wolfmeyer (2014) documents the deep commitments that mathematics education has for the development of human capital, or those intangible qualities usable by businesses.

1.2   STEM education policy critiques

Not young, STEM education policy is historically entrenched with nationalistic goals of militarism and economic security. Within the current context of neoliberal governmentality and multinational corporations, these commitments have made broader turns towards global economic and power elite. Having laid out these commitments and the historical trajectory of STEM, we next review the ways to critique educational policy so as to turn these lenses on STEM education policy.

Education policy critiques encompass large interrelated areas. Many critiques center on exploring the efficiency of the specific policies; others concentrate on uncovering the fallible foundational principles that are used to justify policy decisions. Still others question the covert agendas behind policies, which either intentionally or unintentionally negatively affect minority groups. Most STEM policy critiques to date focus only on the first of these; it is our intention to push the conversation beyond a policy's efficiency in the direction of its foundational principles and covert agendas. Here we will review the efforts made thus far as motivation for our work's complementary place in STEM conversations.

Most critiques on policies' effectiveness question whether the policies, as they are stated, can reach their purported goals. For example, some scholars have argued that there have only been cosmetic changes in mathematics education with no real changes taking place. Reys (2001) asserts that the reason for lack of change in reforms is the difficulty in changing textbooks, which are still the primary teaching tool in schools. Districts that are undergoing financial stress do not have the funds necessary for getting new resources to complement the guidelines certain policies specify. Without the funding, policies become purely rhetorical and have little or no effect on the real day-to-day lives of teachers and students in the classroom (Apple, 2003). Schoenfeld (2004) claims that the National Council of Teachers of Mathematics

(NCTM) and NSF policy standards recommendations have been vague and backed by little or no evidence or research. This is an example of critiques on efficiency that are quite widespread on all ends of the educational debate. The commonality between these critiques of educational policy is that they all expose the problems with the way policies specify how changes will take place.

Speaking more directly to the entirety of STEM, a group of STEM education experts wrote a policy white paper for the National Academy of Education (Kilpatrick, Quinn, and National Academy of Education, 2009). The arguments are similar to those made in the specifics of mathematics education: the enacted national, state and local policies lack the substance for significant change. For example, while paying science and mathematics teachers higher salaries is something that might work, these scholars argue that such changes pale in comparison to complete overhauls of standards at the national level. The build-up of such argumentation by academics has aligned with other political and economic interests (e.g., assessment industry) to usher in national standards for both mathematics and science (Wolfmeyer, 2014). Again, these policy critiques center primarily on the efficacy of policy to address the economic and militaristic imperatives in STEM. Little thus far has critiqued STEM policy on its fundamental terms.

Foundational views could encompass cultural, social, political, and philosophical perspectives. Stigler and Hiebert (2004) express the idea that "implementation cannot be successful unless it is accompanied by ideological and cultural change within schools" (p. 15). What these authors are addressing is the way in which STEM education is related to our cultural perceptions about the uses and values this content has in our society. Take mathematics, for example. If educators and policymakers believe mathematics is a necessary tool for economic prosperity for individual and national gains, they will emphasize the utilitarian aspects of the subject and may ignore the beauty of mathematical proofs and procedures, not to mention the creative and imaginative disposition needed to enjoy and be good at mathematics. Further, if educators and policy makers have not experienced the joy a mathematician feels when attempting to solve a problem, they may not emphasize this kind of aesthetic experience when doing mathematics. Hence, educators and policymakers that either do not appreciate the wonder of mathematics or see it as a means to an economic ends, will interpret and implement policies to reform mathematics education in perhaps different ways than originally intended by the theorists and researchers that have helped shape such reforms.

Therefore, our work here complements other STEM policy analysis by moving beyond arguments related to efficient policy initiatives. We are developing robust analysis that reflect back to fundamental assumptions and presuppositions in the policy that, in turn, moves STEM forward as a hopeful space in which teachers can fully engage. It is worth noting that our work's attention to philosophical methods is entirely within the spirit of developing an informed practice of education.

1.3   Why philosophy of STEM?

This section provides a rationale for why philosophical inquiry can help in understanding educational phenomenon. As we began to suggest in the previous section, this work complements the policy critique work that focuses on policy efficacy. Philosophical method is the application of philosophical concepts to a particular domain of study. It includes the formulation of questions and problems and justifiable solutions to these. It does not occur by collecting and analyzing data on the lived experience, as is the case with a variety of forms of empirical research.

While a great deal has been written about how to meet the objectives of STEM, the work has been limited in methodology, strictly adhering to quantitative analysis, and limited in scope, rarely putting into question the overarching objectives of the policies themselves. Scholars in various fields have critiqued such work. Educational researchers have offered qualitative or more nuanced approaches to better understand the subtleties of STEM initiative implementation (e.g., Lester, 2005; Schmidt, Wang, and McKnight, 2005; Stigler and Hiebert, 2004; Stone, 2002). Social justice scholars critique the STEM initiatives as not targeting embedded social equity issues rhetorically advocated for in the discourse itself (e.g., Apple, 1992; Gabbard, 2000; Martin, 2003; Wolfmeyer, 2014). However, very little has been written targeting the philosophical assumptions inherent in the STEM policies themselves, for example, as they might lend themselves to social injustices. We believe this is a grave mistake since mathematics and science, the foundational knowledge needed in technology and engineering, are both fields deeply entrenched in historical, cultural, and philosophical perspectives. Put another way, those with critical perspectives on education would do well to deeply explore STEM policy, as we hope to here. If we hope to counter balance the neoliberal rhetoric that has so permeated educational policy discourses in the United States, perhaps the best place to start is where the rhetoric is strongest.

Using philosophical inquiry begins with the underscoring of STEM as a discourse, a social construct developed as a response to various events. There has been a plethora of scholarship investigating policy reform packages and the discourse that surrounds them (e.g., Charalambous and Phillippou, 2010; Dejarnette, 2012; Schmidt, 2012). The research can be categorized by two broad agendas: social justice pursuits in order to understand how minority groups can be included in the "STEM pipeline" and pragmatic efforts to ensure school districts and communities have the necessary resources to implement STEM reforms. These distinctive research agendas are indeed important for ameliorative efforts to enhance both individual and national objectives; however, these research agendas are not nearly exhaustive enough to provide useful information for policy makers about mathematics and science education in the United States.

Education policy research is a widespread area of study, especially given the current trends in evaluation, assessment, and efficiency. Due to these trends, most policy research is conducted as *"research for"* policy not *"research of"* policy (italics added, Cross, 2004). *Research for* policy can have the following objectives: (1) to study a specific policy implementation process to assess its effectiveness (e.g., Honig, 2006) or (2) to employ experimental or observational methods for the purpose of recommending specific policy interventions (e.g., Kilpatrick, 2001; Radford, 2006). While these are worthy research agendas, certain assumptions about mathematics and science are often left uncontested. However, it is precisely these disregarded assumptions that are foundational to epistemological claims that underlie pedagogical theories on learning and axiological objectives that specify for what STEM education ought to be used.

Research of policy seeks to understand the explicit and implicit messages embedded within policy documents, in order to enhance, by way of critique, the overall objectives of education policy. This meta-level of analysis is extremely important today due to the complexity and multiple contexts in which education in the United States is situated. Policy, after all, is neither a static entity nor a controlled unmediated practice. Rather it is a process that is struggled over by many different stakeholders at all levels of development and implementation. Ozga (2004) argued that research of policy is an undeveloped field of research, and urges educational researchers to develop rigorous methodological and interdisciplinary approaches for analyzing policy. Concurring with Ozga, Cross (2004) defines *research of* policy as a critique of policy itself insofar as such research is a vital component of the scholarly work needed in a democratic state. He argues that research of policy contributes to the protection of our fragile democratic state by increasing the public awareness of government activities. Moreover, research of policy enables a reflexivity to emerge that allows researchers to ask more complex questions about the purposes of education, and how such purposes can be attained comprehensively through policy initiatives. Again, the relationship between assumptions about STEM content (ontology), claims on best practices of teaching STEM content (epistemology), and aims of STEM policy reforms (axiology), all relate to one another and ought to be investigated for how this relationship is discussed and presented in public policy texts.

Several scholars have engaged in more of what we consider *research of* STEM education policy. Beginning with mathematics, theoretical gaps in mathematics pedagogical practices as advocated by the NCTM Standards and Principles has also been critiqued rigorously through multiple lenses, including examining class, cognition, and race issues (Apple, 1992; Gutstein, 2008; Kelly, 2008; Martin, 2008). Some critical theorists and researchers argue that mathematics education policy has been simplified and appropriated to only serve neoliberal economic objectives, which for them are antidemocratic and lead to furthering the social inequities prevalent in US society (e.g., Frankenstein, 1983; Gutstein, 2006; Skovsmose, 1994).

Similarly, there are a variety of critiques of science education policy. Besides arguments calling for policy emphasis on greater equity in science education, there is increasing attention paid to the notion of putting the learning of science into social context (e.g., Kumar and Chubin, 2000). This is referred to as the science–technology–society (STS) movement, but some suggest it is only a beginning. Hodson (2004) calls for science education policy that politicizes students to action. Other philosophers of science education provide clear critique of policy. For example, Pierce (2012) considers the role that science education plays in the biocapitalist era. Essentially, science education reduces students to natural resources in which investments can be made and profits reaped. By drawing on social theory, specifically Foucault's biocapitalism, he moves significantly beyond the more simple notion of human capital development. However, this work resonates strongly with critiques of mathematics education (e.g., Wolfmeyer, 2014). As these consistent themes across science, mathematics, and technology education emerge, we witness the broader critique of STEM education.

A philosophical perspective is lacking in educational research today, particularly when it comes to *research of* policy. Philosophically oriented scholars of education have asserted that all educational research assumes philosophical commitments (e.g., Biesta, 2010; Bridges and Smith, 2007; Holma, 2010; Phillips, 2007). While work has been done utilizing a philosophical perspective in mathematics and science education scholarship, very little has discussed ontology and even less has analyzed education policy. Ontological inquiry in education is slowly gaining momentum (e.g., Brown, 2010; Cobb et al., 1992; Restivo, Bendegam, and Fischer, 1993). Yet, with the exception of a few scholars (e.g., Bosse, 2006), very little work has analyzed policy specifically for its ontological commitments.

This book fills the gap in educational *research of* policy by inserting a more robust philosophical perspective to analyze STEM education policy. By questioning the underlying conceptualization of STEM's content (mathematics and science, technology, and engineering) itself, its ontological assumptions, research of policy can provide a rich descriptive model of STEM education policy. Such a model provides a more comprehensive framework to critique reform policies as well as suggest alternate ones. By incorporating a philosophical theoretical framework for investigating the ontological assumptions STEM education can posit about the very nature of STEM content, researchers and theorists may be able to ask more complex questions about the way in which STEM as a discipline and as a school subject, can influence societal normative values and the political educational goals that adopt them. In addition, the investigation of policy texts using a philosophical lens opens up a space for potentially new visions of how philosophy of STEM education can play a role in policy discourses and how educators can enact real change in their own classrooms while navigating the education policy landscape that governs how and why they teach STEM.

Searching for a relationship between philosophy, STEM, and education assumes that philosophy has a rightful place in education. This assumption is justified, not only for education in the broad sense, but particularly for STEM, and especially mathematics, since the study of mathematics has been intertwined with philosophy proper dating back to ancient Greece. In Greece, mathematics was thought to be a necessary area of expertise preceding the study of philosophy. In the modern era, important figures in philosophy, such as Charles Peirce, have argued the intrinsic nature of mathematical thinking as being similar in kind to philosophical inquiry (Campos, 2010). Many of the great philosophers of the western philosophical tradition, such as Immanuel Kant, Baruch Spinoza, and Ludwig Wittgenstein, have made use of mathematics as an exemplar to understanding the limits of human knowledge. Indeed, there are separate philosophical fields known as philosophy of mathematics, philosophy of science, and philosophy of technology. Well-known philosophers of science include Karl Popper, Thomas Kuhn, Paul Feyerabend, and Karen Barad. Over time, this field has engaged the notion of the scientific method, initially in support of it as a method for objective study, and more recently in understanding scientific knowledge construction as embedded in cultural and political contexts.

While the disciplines of philosophies of mathematics and science have gone to the background in popular philosophical dialogue, the discipline of philosophy of education has continued to maintain its small yet important influence on educational discourse. This may be because education, especially in the 21st century United States, has become highly visible to the public. However, with all the media coverage of public education, the dominant discourse is still predominantly concerned with direct means and ends of education, such as how best to implement a particular policy and which types of policies are most needed to impact the most good for the largest number of Americans. Thus, it seems that neither philosophy of STEM content nor philosophy of education has a direct impact on policy reform efforts. Nonetheless, these discourses have a significant role to play in critiquing reform efforts and offering alternative ones. This role can be further enhanced by providing a theoretical bridge between the discourses of philosophies of mathematics and science and philosophy of education to the education of STEM. In the next few paragraphs, we will briefly review philosophies of mathematics and science and the initial ways in which they have been applied to science education and mathematics education.

Starting with mathematics, there have been excellent efforts at conceptualizing the relationship between philosophy, education, and mathematics (Ernest, 1994, 2004; Steiner, 1987). There are a variety of approaches. The first schema has popular backing as this oft-cited quote could attest to: "All mathematical pedagogy, even if scarcely coherent, rests on a philosophy of mathematics" (Thom, 1973, p. 204). In this schema all learning theories in education rest on philosophical assumptions, although they can be bound by political agendas as well as social/cultural normative views. Here, epistemic as well as ontological assumptions are the fundamentals for thinking about the best teaching and learning theories for mathematics education. While we immediately gravitate toward this schema as a contender for our convictions for research into mathematics (and STEM) education policy, we are unsure to what extent the philosophical categories of philosophy are used. Since the emphasis here is strictly on philosophy of mathematics as it relates to education, key axiological discourses might be overlooked.

The second schema in philosophy of mathematics education anchors itself in political/ethical concerns in education, which are especially interesting when it comes to mathematics; however, by doing this it can blind itself to other concerns, such as cognition of abstract knowledge and the aesthetic experience so often associated with learning mathematics (e.g., Crannell, 2009; Sinclair, 2001). In this schema, the emphasis is on the political and ethical issues in education, and how these translate to the context of mathematics education. If we assume, as critical theorists do, that mathematics is a field inherent with explicit as well as implicit political agendas, it makes sense to assume a critical stance on its education and begin our critique within a philosophy of education perspective as it relates to mathematics education. Skovsmose's (1994) book *Towards a Critical Philosophy of Mathematics Education* lays an excellent framework for thinking philosophically about the aims and means mathematics education ought to recognize and serve, which for him is always political in nature. Being a critical theorist, Skovsmose contends that power relations are inherent in mathematics and thus its education must serve the ethical and political dimensions of citizens who work toward a free and just democracy.

A more complex perspective of philosophy of mathematics education, one that does not simply cut and paste a particular view of philosophy of education onto mathematics education, comes from Peter Ernest (2004). He suggested that we ought to view philosophy of mathematics education not as a single position, but as "an area of investigation" (p. 1). Traditionally, research in education focused on the practices of teaching and learning of mathematics, such as what cognitive theories best fits mathematics learning objectives and what types of classroom organizations best facilitate learning of mathematics. Philosophical investigations into these traditional areas of research are pertinent, and many scholars (e.g., Cobb et al., 1992) have done useful research, yet the broader societal realm has been left unanalyzed. Philosophical analysis can be put to work in uncovering the broader implications of mathematics education policy. By studying the interrelations through a metanarrative, as well as through a microlevel and bisectional view, we can gain a complex yet more enlightening view about what is really going on in the discourse about mathematics education, which is the objective of this work.

Philosophy of science education is also an emerging field of study, albeit perhaps a bit less developed (there is, e.g., a journal on the philosophy of mathematics education but not a similar one for science). Efforts have been made to consider the relationship science education has with philosophy of science, as in Burbules and Linn (1991). As with mathematics education, there are several scholars using philosophical methods to advance science teaching. Kubli (2010) articulates the need for a philosophy of science education rooted primarily in epistemological claims relating to teaching methods. Similarly, Burgh and Nichols (2012) relate scientific inquiry to philosophical inquiry as a means to bolster science pedagogy. These works present science education with little relation to political and economic contexts, but there are science education scholars who relate philosophical ideas as they move beyond describing pedagogies that exist in vacuums. For example, many scholars argue for the inclusion of socioscientific issues in science education, a concept related to STS. On its own, this work is grounded in philosophy, especially axiological stances for the purposes of education. Moreover, some work has explicitly related this argumentation to philosophical underpinnings. For example, Blades (2006) describes how ethics, a branch of philosophy, can support an STS-focused science education. In this brief review of philosophies of mathematics and science education, we suggest that philosophy's relevance to science and mathematics education is already well articulated, and in so doing this motivates and justifies our philosophical inquiry into STEM education.

1.4 Outline of the book

This chapter reviewed key events in STEM's history up to and including its current status as a dominant global educational discourse. We also provided a rationale for why philosophical inquiry can help understand educational phenomenon and an introduction to ideas contained in the subsequent chapters. Using philosophical inquiry begins with the underscoring of STEM as a discourse, a social construct as a response to various societal circumstances and especially the results of efforts made by those in power. Specific philosophical tools and theories are argued for their relevance as well, including those used in the book's subsequent chapters.

In the next chapter, we use three philosophical tools to examine the STEM discourse. To begin, the use of ontology examines the content areas of STEM. In conceptualizing mathematics, science, engineering, and technology, we review the philosophies of mathematics and science and competing paradigms for technology, and engineering's place in society. Moving to epistemology, we explore theories of knowledge and how they influence theories of teaching and learning within the STEM discourse. Empiricism, rationalism, and constructivism are reviewed as each relates to the STEM content areas but more importantly as it relates to the teaching of STEM. Accordingly, these epistemologies link to pedagogical methods within STEM, from traditional, didactic teaching to constructivist and sociocultural learning, as well as revealing possibilities for pedagogy that challenges society's assumptions and practices. Finally, axiology addresses the purposes of STEM education. Here we review the mainstream value of STEM education, to develop human capital in the continued pursuit of profit-driven consumerism. Drawing upon the work of the entire chapter, STEM axiology, epistemology, and ontology position potentialities for a value set more sympathetic to critical, social reconstructionist schooling.

Chapter 3 describes Alain Badiou's opus as it relates to STEM education. Drawing upon Badiou's work, which centers on a new way of conceptualizing how newness or change can emerge in society, this chapter seeks to describe how Badiou would understand the potentiality for social justice events to occur within the STEM discourse. This understanding can only be achieved by investigating what Badiou terms the "state of the situation," which can be done through a set theoretical analysis of policy documents. Incorporating Alain Badiou's set theory method of analysis, we examine the STEM discourse to understand the complex web that interconnects its inherent subject matter, pedagogy, and purpose (ontology, epistemology, and axiology, respectively). The method fuses mathematical language and method with Badiou's method of educational analysis to further complicate and understand STEM as the world's power elite has produced it. This reveals their mainstream efforts as well as promising spaces, or voids, in which transformative education can occur.

Growing out of earlier contents in the book, the final chapter, Chapter 4 is dedicated fully to exploring the spaces where changes in the STEM discourse have the potential to occur. One such space is the aesthetic ontological appreciation of mathematics, which is a transformative project in which such appreciation contextualizes liberation activities in the Marcusian sense. In redefining what counts as science, ancient ways of knowing the biosphere reveal STEM's potentiality to address social and ecological crises. Similarly, redefining STEM's axiology, ontology, and epistemology of technology and engineering will move these content areas from their present circumstance as "the problem" to one in which they are "the solution."

2
STEM's What, Why, and How? Ontology, Axiology, and Epistemology

Abstract: *In this chapter we use the philosophical concepts of ontology, axiology, and epistemology to understand STEM more completely. We first provide a brief orientation to the history of how these terms have been used in philosophical discourse; then we delve into an overview of these three categories with respect to each subarea of STEM, starting with mathematics and science. In each case we explain how they have historically been implemented in education, and philosophically how they have been utilized to critique and/ or aid inquiry into each subcontent area. In conclusion, we refine the picture by addressing the axiology, epistemology, and ontology of STEM as a singular unit.*

Keywords: axiology; education policy; epistemology; ontology

Chesky, Nataly Z. and Mark R. Wolfmeyer. *Philosophy of STEM Education: A Critical Investigation.* New York: Palgrave Macmillan, 2015. DOI: 10.1057/9781137535467.0007.

The educational acronym "STEM" represents a multidisciplinary education perspective that combines the disciplines of science, technology, and engineering with mathematics. This may be significant since past policy reforms, which were also concerned about the need to maintain global competitiveness, concentrated on mathematics, foreign language, and science education (Klein, 2003). What is unique about STEM is that mathematics and science are no longer enough for knowledge acquisition of a modern citizen, but must be intertwined with technology and engineering. These latter fields differ substantially, for example, from mathematics, which included abstract thinking that does not necessarily apply to practical uses. This turn in policy discourse may imply a crucial turn in the way our society values and teaches students about mathematics and the other disciplines. In this chapter we use the philosophical concepts of ontology, axiology, and epistemology to understand STEM more completely. To begin, this will require analyzing the STEM disciplines each on their own (in particular mathematics and science education). This will provide a background to understand STEM's interdisciplinay content and the way that STEM as a unit complicates each of these content areas. First, however, we review the philosophical terms ontology, epistemology, and axiology in greater detail especially with respect to their application to educational inquiry. Traditionally, philosophy has five branches: metaphysics (ontology—the study of the state of being); logic (the study of reasoning); ethics (axiology—the study of what one ought to do or what is right); aesthetics (the study of beauty, art); and epistemology (the study of knowledge and scope of knowledge).

Figure 2.1 depicts a diagram of three of these philosophical domains and how they can relate to education. We intend it to provide a guide for the philosophical terms we are using throughout this book. Ontology relates to the conceptual assumptions we have about what STEM is about (e.g., for mathematics, what numbers are, how functions and geometric properties interact with the empirical world). Epistemology relates to pedagogical theories as to how best to teach STEM, which are based on a theoretical and/or research-driven approach that claims children learn mathematics, science, engineering, and technology knowledge in a certain way. Axiology relates to objectives of STEM education regarding why children should learn STEM content. These are based on broader normative views as to what STEM knowledge ought to be used for.

In what follows, we first provide a brief orientation in the history of how these terms have been used in philosophical discourse; then we

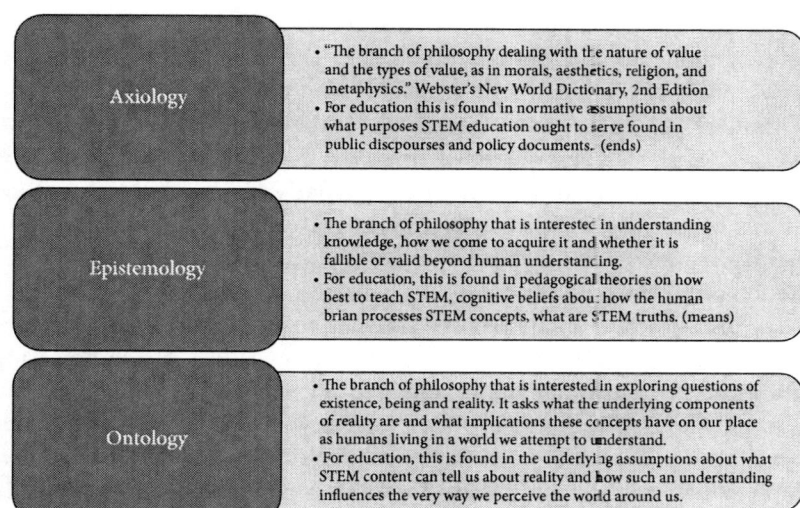

FIGURE 2.1   *Axiology, ontology, and epistemology*

delve into an overview of these three categories with respect to each subarea of STEM, starting with mathematics and science. Technology and engineering are included as an add-on to science; for example, in each section the concept of science and technology studies (STS) is addressed. In this chapter we are drawing primarily on the education research literature that contains far less on technology and engineering education than it does on mathematics and science. We further develop these two areas in the final chapter when we sketch an alternative STEM that draws more broadly from among all philosophical contributions. For now, we explain how they have historically been implemented in education, and philosophically how they have been utilized to critique and/or aid inquiry into each subcontent area. In conclusion, we refine the picture by addressing the axiology, epistemology, and ontology of STEM as a singular unit.

2.1   Ontology: What subjects are we studying?

Ontology inquiries in education require us to determine what subjects we are studying. Accordingly, we question how mathematics, science, and technology are conceptualized in this historical moment: their arrival as the singular unit referred to as STEM. This includes reviews of the philosophies of mathematics and science and competing paradigms for technology's place in society. Mathematics is typically referred to as cut and dry, value-free, and objective; however, it actually refers to a variety of conceptions and human activities. Similarly, we provide competing natures of science (NOS) as described by a variety of philosophers of science. Technology and engineering are folded into this section's introduction of the STS movement.

Beginning with mathematics, conceptions of mathematics relate to both pedagogies of mathematics, and to objectives of mathematics education. Certainly, depending on what the objectives of mathematics education are, pedagogies of mathematics will follow, since curricula decisions are always tied to pedagogical decisions. Unlike epistemology, ontology has been extremely misrepresented in educational research. To be clear, the link between epistemic claims about how we gain mathematical knowledge is only related, but not subsumed and not the same as where we believe such knowledge is located. Although there is an ontological question that always underlies epistemological claims, acquiring knowledge of something is not the same thing as understanding what exactly that knowledge is about. In other words, epistemology, which is interested in how knowledge can be attained, the nature of such knowledge, and the ways in which it can be transmitted (taught/learned) is not the same thing as ontology, which is interested in the object and/or process that knowledge is trying to learn about. For education, this distinction has significant implications.

Whether one posits a purely semiotic view of mathematics as nominalists do or even a purely mental construct game of finite symbols (as intuitionists believe) ontological assumptions are inherent.

Without collapsing into sophistry, a philosophy of mathematics education must rest its theoretical musings on ontological presuppositions in the very least. Rowlands and Carson (2001) use this argument to fervently critique constructivists' approaches to pedagogy in mathematics. They make a rather convincing argument that we cannot escape ontological questions in philosophy of mathematics education since this will lead to a flawed theory of how to teach mathematics. Pragmatics might argue that ontology is irrelevant as long as the theory works in practice. This might be true for other subjects taught in school, but mathematics is intrinsically tied to ontology since it asks us to abstract from symbolic relationships possible values of unknown entities.

There are traditionally two ways of conceptualizing the field of mathematics. These can be understood as the dichotomy between absolutist and fallibilist notions of mathematics, where the former believes mathematics has a direct link to empirical or rational truths outside the human subject, while the latter posits that all mathematical knowledge is based on cultural, social, and political forces that are inherently flawed, evolving, and biased. Absolutist includes realism and some forms of formalism and intuitionism. Fallibilist includes nominalism and constructivism (Ernest, 2004). Absolutism includes Formalism, Logicism, and to a certain extent Intuitionism and fallibilistic includes Nominalism, Constructivism. Fallibilistic accounts (e.g., Davis and Hersh, 1980; Ernest, 1994, 2004; Lakatos, 1976; Tymoczko, 1993) view mathematics as a humanistic discipline that is an outcome of social processes. Absolutism views mathematical knowledge as a direct by-product of either deductive rational inquiry or empirical validation depending on where mathematical entities are posited (either mental or empirical). Certainty, these theoretical conceptions of mathematics rest upon epistemological views on how we gain access to mathematics knowledge and ontological views that suggest of what reality is made.

This simplistic dichotomy leaves much to be desired. Whether or not we posit an ontological status for mathematical truths, it is unclear how pedagogical practices ought to be affected. Indeed, neither seems very satisfactory given the complexity of the debates in current philosophy of mathematics discourses. Further, each camp seems to argue for their own view by critiquing the others or ignoring them altogether. Fallibilists ignore the paradigmatic paper given by Eugene Wigner, a mathematician, titled "the unreasonable usefulness of mathematics" (Burbaker, 2008). By ignoring the empirical uses that mathematical abstraction continues to play in science, fallibilistic accounts of mathematics loses tremendous credibility. On the other hand, by ignoring Kuhn's theories on paradigm shifts, such as the fallibility of Euclidean geometry, which is now unanimously agreed by professional mathematicians and scientists, absolutism accounts of mathematics appear stubbornly rigid and illogical.

A third possibility is what we have termed aesthetic conceptions of mathematics. Scholars (e.g., Crannell, 2009; Sinclair, 2001; Tymoczko, 1993; Wang, 2001) have proclaimed the aesthetic dimension of mathematics as the key characteristic of the mathematical learning experience. Indeed, great mathematicians from Poincare to Godel have asserted that their practice of mathematics is latent with aesthetical experiences (Devlin, 2000). Even the National Council of Teachers of Mathematics (NCTM) asserts that a connection to art and music ought to be achieved in the mathematics classroom. Two examples of a philosophy of mathematics based on aesthetics are Resnik's (1981) notion of mathematics as a study of patterns and Shapiro's (1997) mathematics as a study of structures. Within these views, mathematicians and philosophers of mathematics are not concerned with the ontological properties or truth-values of numbers themselves, but only the structures and relationships that bind them together. Thus, the absolutism claim that numbers exist outside of human understanding as well as the fallibilistic assertion that numbers are completely part of a human cultural understanding of a particular worldview, make way for an alternative. This alternative is not a compromise or a synthesis of the two more popular dichotomous views, but an altogether new ontological conception of mathematics.

A simple way of understanding this is to realize that numbers are always in relation to one another. For example, you are only short compared to someone taller; a thousand dollars is either a lot of money or not that much depending on where you live and the lifestyle you are accustomed to. The question is how does this conception of mathematics relate to an aesthetic ontological perspective? We should remember that ontology attempts to explain the parts or reality; in mathematics, ontology attempts to explain the nature of numbers, mathematical operations, and processes. It is how this ontological perspective translates to the experiences of doing mathematics that can also be viewed as aesthetic. Mathematicians discuss the creative process of working on a proof and the inductive nature of mathematics, which necessitates a recursive type of thinking and an intuitive sense that what one is doing may yield new knowledge to the field. Conceiving numbers as relations, rather than static entities or culturally meaningless terms, may elicit a more aesthetic experience in the practice of doing mathematics. This has great implications for education, especially at the elementary level when numbers are first introduced.

How do these three conceptions of mathematics compare to the meta-discourses discussed of ontology, epistemology, and axiology? First, we can say that epistemology and ontology are explicitly given precedents in absolutism and fallibilist accounts of mathematics. This might not be explicit in aesthetical conception of mathematics since the model we borrow from Resnik does not clearly define an ontological referent to the patterns mathematics is supposed to study. Instead, Resnik contends that patterns or relationships are all that exists, which by itself we claim is an ontological view. Clearly, we can say, pedagogy will be conceived drastically different depending on which view of mathematics one holds, although as we will see in the following section, this may be an incorrect assumption.

Ethically, there may be a specific dilemma that emerges within any given account of mathematics once it is put into the politically charged education system. Certainly, democratic ideals would change from absolutist and fallibilist accounts of mathematics since these assume different axiological objectives for mathematics education and thereby change the discourse in education policies. As the editors of *Math Worlds* contend, "mathematics itself is an expression of social relations" (Restivo, Bendegam, and Fischer, 1993, p. 15). Thus, the way we conceptualize mathematics directly relates to how we interact on a political and social level. It would seem then that the three internal discourses are linked by conceptions of mathematics since this one relates to pedagogies as well as objectives of education. Mathematics, as it is traditionally taught and conceived of as an absolutist account, causes us to assume the world is made up of quantifiable entities. This belief allows us to construct objective standards with which to measure ourselves and to place value on such knowledge. On the other hand, if one assumed a fallibilist account of mathematics and utilized constructivist or political pedagogical approaches, our worldview might be altered in that we would not seek to determine value based on quantifiable measures.

Lastly, entertaining an aesthetic conception of mathematics, ontologically the topic becomes very interesting. Thinking about mathematics as a discipline that attempts to understand patterns and relationships provides an alternative to the historical aim of education as well as the pedagogies that have come forth to meet them. Here, mathematics education would aim to provide an aesthetic experience of doing mathematics, which would in turn inspire the imagination and bring forth the necessary cognitive apparatus needed to learn mathematics well. In addition, and this is our most far reaching claim, if we learn mathematics as a system of relations and patterns, our ways of conceptualizing our world and ourselves might change as well so that we would view connections to be explored rather than quantities to be measured.

Turning to the ontology of science education, we will review philosophies of science as we did with mathematics. In looking at some of the major philosophers of science, we will see that philosophy of science follows a similar trajectory to mathematics, where certainty and objective truth are asserted in modern thinking and problematized later on. Again, by looking at the ontology of science we aim to uncover the way that scientific knowledge helps us to come to know about and live in the world.

A common starting point in the philosophy of science comes with a look at Descartes' *Discourse on Method* first published in 1637. Essentially spelling out what we have all learned as the scientific method in formal schooling, this is representative of the rationalistic view of modern science. It leads to the notion that what we learn through the method is true, correct, objective, and value-free. We now understand the method to be a blind faith in a process that is almost always entirely embedded within subjectivities and political/economic contexts.

One clear uprising against such dogma was Kuhn's (1962) *The Structure of Scientific Revolutions*. In this highly popular and influential work, Kuhn identifies the occurrence of scientific paradigms, in which significant ideas put forth by the scientific community necessitate overhauls of previous scientific thought. When a new paradigm emerges, the scientific community responds and reacts to reaffirm the new paradigm and reject the old. Although Kuhn's paradigm does not entirely negate scientific method or come close to asserting that science lacks truth or objectivity, it does suggest the social nature of scientific knowledge making and exposes an element of irrationality to the process. In other words, he clearly suggests that scientific concept generation is not simply a process of simple inquiry and data collection, but rather something deeply embedded in social engagements.

When it comes to philosophers of science, the staunchest opposition to classical method comes from Paul Feyerabend. With titles like *Against Method* (1975) and *Farewell to Reason* (1987) it is clear where he stands. Among the major points in his writings is the rejection that scientific knowledge is produced within a strict, universal methodology, such as described by Descartes. Furthermore, he argues that scientists are restricted if forced to operate entirely within this method and should instead be free to work outside of this. In addition, Feyerabend applied anarchism (freedom from authority and hierarchy) to scientific knowledge production. Notably Feyerabend also argued against science's supreme status in *Science in a free society* (1982), a notion of particular interest to an inquiry in STEM education given its priority in education policy reform. Feyerabend considers western science to be one of several traditions by which we can understand and live in the world. He rejects the elitist stance scientists take over other ways of knowing. In all cases Feyerabend rejects the notion that science is objective truth.

Thomas Kuhn and Paul Feyerbend are philosophers of science that study the context of scientific knowledge production. This is sometimes understood as the sociology of scientific knowledge and overlaps with the notion of STS referred to in Chapter 1 of this book. In this line of thinking, what becomes clear is the way that scientific knowledge production is embedded in historical, political, and economic contexts. To varying degrees, these philosophers of science reject the objectivity of scientific knowledge and instead favor the ways that science functions within and for societal goals. These are important points to consider as we inquire into STEM education, especially when public and political understandings of scientific knowledge have not yet reached this level of scrutiny. Along these lines and as we will see in Chapter 4, becoming conscious of the way societal traditional gender roles have influenced the way in which we make sense of our world has not only limited our scientific knowledge, but all of our human endeavors (Lloyd, 1995).

Having looked at both philosophies of mathematics and science, we see several overlaps in the way they have evolved over time. This has significant implications as we understand and critique STEM as a unit. The modern view of mathematics and science suggests these as objective, value-free knowledges that are produced without context. Their goals are to seek truth via rational means. As to be demonstrated in Chapter 3, the public and those in political and economic power embrace this view of science and mathematics. Indeed bringing STEM together as a singular unit is indicative of such dogmatic belief in the two disciplines. However, further advancements in our understanding of these, as reviewed in the above philosophies of science and mathematics, demonstrate a consistent arc for both mathematics and science in which we must reject such claims to superior knowledge, truth, and objectivity. The fallibalism in philosophy of mathematics resonates with the movement to ascertain the sociology of scientific knowledge.

2.2 Epistemology: How can we learn STEM?

In turning next to epistemology, we ask, "How can we learn STEM?" Here we explore theories of knowledge and how they influence theories of teaching and learning within the STEM discourse. To begin, theories of knowledge include empiricism, rationalism, and constructivism. Each is reviewed as it relates to the STEM content areas of mathematics and science but more importantly as it relates to the teaching of STEM. Accordingly, these epistemologies link to pedagogical methods within STEM, from traditional, didactic teaching to constructivist and sociocultural learning. Finally, some epistemological negotiations reveal possibilities for pedagogy that challenges society's assumptions and practices.

In this section we examine the various learning theories that have influenced the teaching and learning of STEM education. As with the ontology section, we will review these theories with both mathematics and science. Thus we describe the dominant voices in the literature on mathematics and science pedagogy. We have differentiated these theories on learning mathematics and science into three broad categories: traditional, constructivist, and transformative. We will not devote much space to traditional teaching of mathematics and science. This is an approach most are familiar with and resembles direct instruction of mathematics/science concepts and skills. In the constructivist approach, for mathematics we will review what is often termed reform mathematics pedagogy and, for science, teaching science through inquiry. Finally, in transformative mathematics pedagogy we review critical mathematics education and in transformative science teaching we include the science-technology studies movement and the teaching of socioscientific issues (SSI).

We begin with the epistemology of mathematics. While science has been proven wrong at times, history is written through biases, and literature can be Eurocentric, mathematics has only in the last century been questioned as not a complete error-proof body of knowledge.[1] Therefore, mathematics is the last school subject to lose its solid unquestionable stance on truth. Of course, it is difficult to gauge the general public's awareness of this trend in philosophy of mathematics and it is perhaps more difficult to understand how this idea has surfaced in philosophy of mathematics education. Traditionally, mathematics was taught as a static body of knowledge and unquestionable truth. However, recently policy discourses have implicitly disagreed with this claim (Sriraman and English, 2010). What is unclear in mathematics education policy is the distinct epistemological stance to support these positions. The reason for this shortcoming may be a lack of philosophical understanding or an unwillingness to be forthcoming with a position that may be unpopular.

Drawing from Vygotsky's dynamic social theory and perhaps Piaget's psychological theory of learning, constructivist pedagogies are extremely influential in the discourses in mathematics education. In fact, the National Council of Teachers of Mathematics (NCTM) explicitly advocated constructivists' methods in teaching mathematics in their 2011 Standards and Guidelines (Kelly, 2008). The aims here seem to be more progressive and child centered; however, pragmatists' aims are also often implicated since alongside constructivist pedagogy, NCTM and other policy initiatives claim that such practices will help students learn the valuable mathematics knowledge they need to get a job. Constructivists' pedagogies are often acclaimed in the literature on mathematics education. Constructivists' pedagogies fall within two camps: radical and social constructivism. Generally, we can say that both constructivist pedagogies deny the classic correspondence theory of truth, which states that humans can have access to external truths. Both approaches claim learning is not a passive activity since the learner must construct all knowledge through direct experience with new information that must interact with already held knowledge to create new cognitive understandings about how the world works (Irzig, 2000). What is unclear is where exactly the knowledge that the child actively constructs is found. This is where social and radical constructivism differs significantly.

Social constructivists (e.g., Kilpatrick, 2001; Hersh, 1993; Valero, 2004) believe knowledge is acquired through the social realm by consensus in a community of inquiries, be they mathematicians or students in a classroom. Radical constructivists (e.g., von Glasersfeld, 1991), on the other hand, strictly say that knowledge can only be created through the subjective process internal to the learner himself. Constructivists claim that theirs is a

> theory of learning and not a theory of knowing, that it is a psychological theory about how beliefs are developed rather than what makes beliefs true, that it makes no ontological claim concerning the external world and that it is "post-epistemological". (Rowlands and Carson, 2001; cites Matthews 1998)

But, as we have already pointed out earlier, all pedagogical theories must rest upon epistemological assumptions; to disregard this claim is to cause undue ambiguity that disparaged the pedagogical objectives themselves. After all, without a clear theory on knowledge, how can one expect to come to have access to it much less an understanding? Social constructivists claim that knowledge is content specific and negotiated through socially mediated activities. But how does this explain the practice of applied mathematics as Eugene Wigner so eloquently wrote about in his famous essay "The unreasonable effectiveness of mathematics." Moreover, how can constructivist pedagogies offer clear methods for learning mathematics, a body of knowledge that has been developing for centuries, in a span of a typical mathematics lesson?

Social constructivism claims parallel Vygotsky's theories on learning; however, their epistemological claims overextend into vague philosophical terrain that causes undue difficulty. Vygotsky himself never endorsed such a radical break from ontological orthodoxy. Neither did Piaget, certainly, who believed biological components had a large role to play in the learning process. Generally, we can say that both constructivist pedagogies deny the classic correspondence theory of truth, which states that humans can have access to external truths. Perhaps they would say it is not that ontological reality does not exist outside of our minds, but only that we cannot have access to it. This philosophical claim is not supported by transcendentalism or any other coherent theory, although, thus some scholars have argued that constructivism merely dissolves itself into solipsism (Rowlands and Carson, 2001; cite Chalmers, 1982). Further, "constructivist activities aim to answer the 'so what?' questions for students, but do so within the given conceptual scheme, taking for granted the ontological primacy of mathematics" (de Freitas, 2004, p. 260; cites Popkewitz, 1998, p. 28). This is a severe drawback since mathematics is very much an abstract creative discipline that can be difficult for many to learn. Perhaps the difficulties in learning lie not in theorizing alternative pedagogical techniques, but in envisioning how ontological conceptions of mathematics influence the way in which students come to learn higher-level mathematics.

Due to social constructivism's loose philosophical foundation, there are several consequences for the mathematics classroom. Consider this strong argument against constructivist theories:

> "If knowledge is nothing more than what is constructed by the individual, then the learner is never wrong—whatever has been constructed has made sense and whatever makes sense is knowledge! If truth is whatever the learner considers to be the case, then there is no body of knowledge, no 'subject-matter' that can be taught as such." (Rowlands and Carson, 2001, p. 3)

How can it be possible to attain a high level of understanding of the richness of mathematics if one cannot be shown where and why certain mathematical operations have been done incorrectly? Wittgenstein aside, students would be quite perplexed if their teacher proclaimed that two plus five did not equal seven. Certainly, philosophical reflection on number existence has a place even in elementary mathematics learning, but this requires a teacher who is well versed in different ontological theories in mathematics.

Radical constructivism fares no better than social constructivist theories for educational practices. This is because algorithms in mathematics—although cognitive construction of mathematical procedures that work arose from many different people through many different ways—converged their expertise to form a consensus as to what constitutes correct computational skills in mathematical practice, and this consensus was not formed by accident, but by application to how the procedures best fit empirical evidence and abstract proofs that stood the test of expert mathematicians of the times. To stress, mathematical practices did not happen by accident and to expect children to form their own algorithms without giving them the necessary deep cognitive understanding of the field of mathematics is time wasting at best and absurd at worst. Another drawback to this approach is that the teacher in radical constructivism is reduced to a mere "facilitator" who has little expert advice to bestow on the children entrusted in his or her care. This role is particularly damaging given the recent efforts towards dismantling teachers' unions and the public's seeming disdain for the "bad teachers" in America; it is damaging to reduce a teacher to a facilitator, since such a role could be played by a software program or anyone not specifically trained in democratic and pedagogical aspects of the professional field of being an educator. In addition, democratic ideals seem to be completely ignored or at least simplified to only being about providing access to knowledge. But since this knowledge is not explicitly linked to empirical reality and only vaguely linked to individual or societal subjective spaces, democratic praxis is practically impossible in this learning theory.

It seems straightforward to connect constructivism to fallibilist notions of mathematics, since knowledge is not seen as universal truth, but rather created by social and individual contexts embedded within societal and cultural spheres. Constructivism differs from traditional pedagogies, which favor an absolutist view of mathematics. More complicated is to ask how the aesthetic conception of mathematics complements or opposes these two pedagogies. At first glance, a constructivist's classroom would seem to foster a more aesthetic experience; however, if mathematical knowledge is believed to be strictly socially construed, certain important, dare we say mysterious, components of mathematics are lost. For instance, students without fail are enthralled when we bring up transcendental numbers in one of our classrooms. Activities may include counting the petals of a daisy, or figuring out the reproduction of rabbits (classic Fibonacci problem showcase the infamous Fibonacci series as it relates to natural phenomena). We also measure our own bodies to investigate its beautiful number proportions and "discover" pi by dividing the circumference by the diameter of any given circle. These lessons would lose their aesthetic appeal if they were somehow reduced to just being about knowledge created by human societies, rather than being about how mathematics can show us intrinsic patterns that occur in nature and in ourselves.

Moving to science, we review a rather similar pedagogy rooted in constructivist theory. The science education research community, including the National Science Teachers Association (NSTA), has promoted teaching science through inquiry for several years. In their standards document, NSTA describes inquiry science as follows:

> "Scientific inquiry reflects how scientists come to understand the natural world, and it is at the heart of how students learn. From a very early age, children interact with their environment, ask questions, and seek ways to answer those questions. Understanding science content is significantly enhanced when ideas are anchored to inquiry experiences." (NSTA, 2004)

Interestingly, this research community shows beginning support of newer philosophies of science, rather than the more traditional, modern forms that emphasize rational process to discover objective truths about the natural world. Among NSTA's declarations of teaching through inquiry, is the following suggestion that multiple methods, not just a rigid scientific method, can lead to scientific discovery: "That there is no fixed sequence of steps that all scientific investigations follow. Different kinds of questions suggest different kinds of scientific investigations" (ibid.) In other words, the science education research community is supportive of thinking about the variety of methods used in science and thus embraces more advanced understandings of scientific knowledge production.

Teaching science through inquiry does not reside entirely within the United States; inquiry is the dominant modality for science teaching across the globe. In *Inquiry in Science Education: International Perspectives* scholars discuss the various contexts in which such teaching occurs. It is clear that international scholars of science inquiry embrace some advancement in philosophy of science as well as constructivist learning theory, similar to the mathematics education research community. For example, writes Niaz (2004): "Discussions of inquiry cannot, at least presently, be divorced from discussions of constructivism, which necessarily bring along issues related to NOS [nature of science]" (p. 406). Niaz acknowledges the disagreements regarding philosophies of science (similar to those outlined in the ontology section above) and also documents what aspects of the nature of science are agreed upon by the science education research community:

> "(a) scientific knowledge is tentative, (b) there is no universal scientific method, (c) theories do not become laws with the accumulation of supporting evidence, (d) scientific activities are theory-laden, (e) scientific knowledge relies on observation, rational arguments, creativity, and skepticism, and (f) scientific ideas are affected by their social and historical milieu. It is noteworthy that these consensus aspects do not explicitly confront controversial issues, such as the nature of reality or the ontological status of scientific concepts." (Niaz, 2004, p. 406)

As Niaz suggests, science education as inquiry embraces constructivist learning theory, making it similar to the mathematics education community's dominant pedagogic framework. And like the mathematics education community, constructivist science teaching resonates with certain advancements in thinking about science, like that of Kuhn's paradigms in which differing approaches to science are understood and the social aspect of scientific knowledge production is acknowledged. However, as Niaz notes, the science education research community's notion of teaching science through inquiry does not embrace full critiques of scientific method, and certainly not Feyerabend's suggestion that science is but one of many ways of knowing the world. Indeed such limitations are seen in NSTA's position statement on inquiry science. The science education research community maintains a commitment to rational thinking and the elitism of scientific knowledge. For example, in stating "That the scientific community, in the end, seeks explanations that are empirically based and logically consistent" (NSTA, 2004) they reiterate the rhetoric so often used to justify science's value to exceed that of other ways of knowing.

In both mathematics and science education communities, we see consistent themes regarding a dominant pedagogic framework resting on constructivist learning theory. Such a situation likely points to both communities embrace of advanced philosophies of mathematics and science. Constructivist learning theory resonates more strongly with the idea that mathematics and science knowledge are social constructions rather than objective realities discovered by humans. However, in both communities the more controversial ontologies of mathematics and science need further exploration. In bringing science and mathematics together as the STEM unit, we suggest that these communities will coalesce to be open to thinking about mathematics and science as social construction but less considerate of placing these knowledges among, rather than above, the other ways of knowing. In other words, the STEM unit considers itself a dominant force among knowledges.

Besides the traditional and constructivist approaches, a third epistemological alternative that has influenced pedagogical theory and research can be termed transformative pedagogy. This alternative is different from constructivist and traditional approaches to teaching and learning mathematics and science, since it assumes at the forefront that power relations are at the core of mathematical and scientific activities and therefore must be made explicit in the education of mathematics. Transformative mathematics and science pedagogies concentrate on not only exposing the power relations that these knowledges hold in a society, but also utilize such power to transform a learner into a critical agent of change within the society. In what follows, we describe two transformative pedagogies for mathematics, ethnomathematics and critical mathematics pedagogy, and two for science, the teaching of SSI and STS.

Ethnomathematics is a pedagogy that stresses that mathematical knowledge was generated in the continual context of cultural history (D'Ambrosio, 2001). In this sense, ethnomathematics is a political and ethical theory of pedagogy that attempts to resist hegemonic Euro-western ideology in order to reestablish epistemological alternatives that are found in indigenous cultures. Ethnomathematics certainly has much to offer, in that it broadens our cultural awareness of indigenous cultures, critiques western positivists claims on mathematics knowledge, and ethically puts into question how mathematics has historically marginalized certain groups of people.

In terms of pedagogical theories, ethnomathematics may be more of a curricula framework than a theory of teaching and learning. Thus, both types of constructivism as explained above could complement ethnomathematics nicely since neither is interested in ontological assumptions but rather strictly considered with epistemology. Traditional pedagogy would be the antithesis to this approach since it assumes that knowledge is stagnant and universal, both claims which ethnomathematics disagrees with. To relate ethnomathematics to conceptions of mathematics, a link can be made with aesthetic conceptions of mathematics. Ron Eglash (2002) is a mathematician who studied villages in South Africa and found that they were constructed with a sophisticated understanding of fractal mathematics; not only this, but when he spoke to the villagers, they were completely aware of the mathematics behind the construction and could explain the mathematical properties in extremely high degrees of mathematics comprehension.

Ethnomathematics claims a fallibilist ontology, yet it is unclear if the knowledge is strictly culturally produced and as such how can it say which system of mathematics ought to be taught other than the one that is currently dominant in the western modern world? Here, ethical pursuits seem most pertinent to ethnomathematics agenda. By trying to show the importance of other culturally known mathematics knowledge, ethnomathematics attempts to provide an empathic view of globally diverse systems of knowledge, with the hope that such information would facilitate a deeper awareness of global problems in the mathematics learner.

The weakness with this educational alternative is that it rests on little epistemological support or ontologically clears assumptions, and is not grounded on any specific political agenda. Katz (1995) argues the epistemological incoherence in ethnomathematics, since there has been historical proof that mathematical "discovers" have arisen in separate locations; for example the Chinese and the Greeks independently figured out the Pythagorean theorem and Pascal's triangle. Further, ethnomathematics does not take into account the political and historical events that have led to the marginalization of certain knowledge over others. For instance, teaching urban US students about African villages does little to give them an understanding of how and perhaps why such villages have been colonized and continue to be places of intense human hardship. More to the point, teaching villagers in Ethiopia about their own culture's contributions to the mathematics discipline lends little real support in their political and personal struggles of survival in a globally connected world that is dominated by a western view of mathematics (Skovsmose, 2006).

Ethnomathematics may serve as a corollary to mathematics education, but it cannot be substituted in any way to the larger growing body that is the western known mathematics discipline, neither for pedagogical gains nor political gains. On the other hand, aesthetic aspects of ethnomathematics could add considerably to the learning experience of students. A more direct link between the transformative pedagogy and education is made with critical mathematics pedagogy.

Critical mathematics pedagogy (e.g., Frankenstein, 1983; Gutstein, 2006; Skovsmose, 1994) was inspired by the work of Paulo Freire, who proclaimed that revolutionary leaders must also be educators. Freire's epistemology is antithetical to the western positivist paradigm in that it views mathematics knowledge and education as never neutral; rather than a set of value-free objective truths, mathematics is seen as creating power relations among different groups of people and then legitimizing these dichotomies to serve the needs of a powerful ruling class. Hence, this pedagogy can be viewed as a fallibilist notion of mathematics, since it assumes power is created and controlled by an elite class and by changing the way in which mathematical power is conceptualized such power relations can be overthrown. We do not see an aesthetic correlation unless we can argue that fostering a political agency is an aesthetic experience. However, we do see a direct relationship to radical constructivism since the individual gains access to knowledge directly, which may harness the critical "consciousness" critical pedagogues hope to achieve in the classroom. What is interesting for modern education of mathematics is that Freire saw how "massified" consciousness is more prevalent in technological societies such as ours and is a major factor in determining the inability of subjugated people to actively engage in their own revolutionary agendas. Thus, developing critical mathematics pedagogy becomes increasingly urgent as our society becomes even more technologically saturated. Skovsmose (2006) expressed that "mathematics education also tends to contribute to the regeneration of an inequitable society through undemocratic and exclusive pedagogical practices" (p. 3).

Critical mathematics pedagogy strives to empower students by enabling them to gain the tools needed to "read the world," and thus have the ability to transform it (Atweh, 2007, p. 7). Unfortunately, there has been no empirical proof that there is a causal relationship between one becoming aware of social inequalities and then becoming politically active in order to bring about change. The possible reason for this disconnect may be due to failing to question hard enough the epistemological and ontological assumptions inherent in how mathematics is perceived. Brantlinger (2011a, 2011b) began his own academic career as an action researcher who passionately believed in critical mathematics pedagogy and used it in an urban classroom to empower his students. However, during the course of his research, Brantlinger became increasingly skeptical of critical mathematics perspective. He writes:

> "Although I see benefits to critical pedagogy, I am wary of critical and other utilitarian versions of school mathematics that explicitly or implicitly eschew value of disciplinary-focused school mathematics... it is essential that critical educators better understand the powerful gatekeeper role that school mathematics serves before we reconceptualize school mathematics as a critical literacy for some students." (2011b, p. 98)

Among other research projects Brantlinger worked on, his textual analysis of textbooks found that the critical mathematics agenda is problematic in terms of equity in urban districts in the United States (2011a).

As arguments previously presented, ontological assumptions are inherently presupposed by certain epistemological stances, which thereby dictate democratic ideas. Concretely, we can say that a positivistic/empirical stance corresponds to an ontological view that there are indeed certain entities, in mathematics, that might mean abstract universal concepts of numbers that are outside human social construction. Inversely, if we take a more formalist or nominalist approach to mathematics, this would garner a view that mathematical knowledge does not exist apart from its historical social context. Positing these two extremes for democratic activism can lead to drastically different results. We believe the disconnect between learning to be mathematics literate and then engaging in praxis to make the world a more just and peaceful place lies in the inability of critical mathematics pedagogy to provide a concrete understanding of how mathematics itself frames our world and how we can use it to reformulate it in our own design. This type of understanding, of course, also needs a high cognitive knowledge of mathematics as well as an imaginative potential that can be fostered by aesthetic experiences in the mathematics classroom.

Transformative pedagogies are important to discuss since they often are the product of a particular critical stance to philosophy of mathematics education. Moreover, they evoke an ethical appeal to democratic objectives that are often missed in both traditional and constructivists' pedagogies. Transformative pedagogies, as do constructivist pedagogies, seem to also fall within the fallibilist camp of mathematics. This seems unproblematic, until we ask if there is a consequence to ignoring the other two conceptions of mathematics.

Moving to transformative science teaching, there are examples of science teaching that situate along a spectrum of social change. On the one hand, there are attempts to democratize scientific knowledge by making it more accessible to the population, including women and people of color. In many cases, this does not explicitly conflict with the human capital development inherent in STEM education policies. In many cases, this work is rationalized for its development of human capital. Thus, this work attends to issues of racial and gender justice without addressing significantly the issues of economic and political power that create injustice. Examples of this kind of work include the admirable progress made in applying culturally relevant pedagogy to science teaching (e.g., Laughter and Adams, 2012). We argue this kind of teaching as transformative because it does address injustices in class, race, and gender, albeit without naming the primary sources of such injustices.

Another trend in the science education research community is its push for the inclusion of SSI in science curricula. This is seen in the United States and international community. For example, Turkey recently included SSI into its national science education standards (Topcu et al., 2014). SSI has grown out of the science—technology—society movement of the 1970s that influenced science education. STS typically

> "stresses the impact of decisions in science and technology on society [but] it does not mandate explicit attention to the ethical issues contained within choices about means and ends, nor does it consider the moral or character development of students." (Zeidler et al, 2005, p. 359)

On the other hand, SSI takes this direction further by providing frameworks for moral and character development through science education. SSI "considers how controversial scientific issues and dilemmas affect the intellectual growth of individuals in both personal and societal domains" (ibid., p. 361). SSI clearly places scientific knowledge in the realm of social contexts, as understood by the sociology of scientific knowledge. This teaching is transformative because it asks students to consider the ways that scientific knowledge can be applied to controversial issues, such as climate change.

There are interesting points to consider with SSI as well. SSI does commit to a social constructivist position of scientific knowledge;

however, it remains highly committed to the superiority of scientific knowledge over other ways of knowing. The ultimate goal of SSI is for students to develop a functional scientific literacy in which scientific inquiry processes can aid in decision making; the subtext here is that such literacy should come at the expense of other ways of knowing about the world. Finally, as noted by Hodson (2004) STS and SSI can be pushed further to encourage students to take political action:

> "It almost goes without saying that science education should lay the foundation for further study and for a potential career as a scientist, engineer, or technician, but it should also be concerned with enabling young citizens to look critically at the society we have, and the values that sustain it, and to ask what can and should be changed in order to achieve a more socially just democracy and to ensure more environmentally sustainable lifestyles." (2004, p. 2)

In bringing together science and mathematics, the STEM unit can engage with the advanced pedagogies of the individual research communities. As reviewed in this section, these include constructivist and transformative pedagogies. In embracing constructivist learning theory, both science and mathematics pedagogies are rooted in epistemological orientations towards the social construction of STEM content knowledge, knowledge that is deeply embedded in political and economic realities. Taking this to its logical conclusion are the transformative pedagogies in both domains, and further embracing of advanced philosophies of science and mathematics (e.g., the inclusion of Feyerabend) would take the transformative pedagogies for STEM to the next level.

2.3 Axiology: Why are we learning STEM?

This section reviews mainstream and alternative values of STEM education. The mainstream view of STEM, created, disseminated, and supported by the world's power elite seeks to develop human capital in the continued pursuit of profit-driven consumerism. Drawing upon the work of preceding sections, the STEM content and pedagogy also reveal potentialities for a value set more sympathetic to critical, social reconstructionist schooling. These include education for aesthetic appreciation and social and environmental justice.

Axiological inquiry has traditionally encompassed ethical issues in education and concentrates on the teacher/student relationship or other classroom-specific dimensions, but this is not our current interest, which is to understand the link between society and STEM. Philosophical discourses on ethics in STEM have also brought up the historical ties of the field (Fried, 2007). For example, we know that mathematics since antiquity has been integral to many of humankind's greatest accomplishments and most deplorable acts (D'Ambrosio, 2001). STEM is deeply entrenched with societal values and concerns. As with the previous sections of this chapter, we will first review mathematics and science education separately, this time looking for the axiological critiques discussed in the literature. Out of this emerge some parallels that suggest an axiological critique of the mainstream STEM unit, thereby providing the impetus for alternative values for STEM.

Beginning with mathematics, Ernest (2004, p. 6) identifies five discrete aims of mathematics education:

1. Industrial Trainer aims: "back to basics," numeracy and social training in obedience (authoritarian).
2. Technological Pragmatists aims: useful mathematics to the appropriate level and knowledge and skill certification (industry centered).
3. Old Humanist aims: transmission of the body of mathematical knowledge (mathematics centered).
4. Progressive Educators aims: creativity, self-realization through mathematics (child centered).
5. Public Educator aims: critical awareness and democratic citizenship via mathematics (social justice centered).

We collapse these five into three categories: utilitarian, cognitive, and democratic aims of education, so that we can better differentiate the aims of mathematics education as they currently exist in current reform discourses. Utilitarian aims can encompass the first two of Ernest's categories, since the commonality is that mathematics education ought to provide the skills and knowledge needed for a productive adult life. Cognitive aims assume that only learning high levels of mathematics ought to be the central import for education, thus this category relates best with the humanist aim, but, we will argue, the progressive aims may fit as well since these are also interested in the direct learning comprehension of the mathematics student. Democratic aims for education may also include progressive aims, but most certainly include the social justice aims.

To give some concrete examples, utilitarian aims of mathematics education can be seen more concretely in reforms such as the America Competes Act that asks schools to produce workers with the technological knowledge our nation needs to maintain its competitive edge in the global marketplace. Utilitarian aims also can be depicted by the Workforce Readiness Taskforce, which wants schools to produce competent future workers. In addition, the call for private corporations to become increasingly involved in education is a direct result of utilitarian objectives in education reforms. In one study, mathematics education's primary purpose is for the development of human capital. Wolfmeyer (2014) indicates this clearly through his robust analysis of the social network of individuals and organizations behind US national mathematics education. The primary interest in this network is the development in people of the intangible qualities usable by businesses, and most other interests in the policy network (such as the testing industry) support these efforts.

Cognitive aims are represented through the "Back to Basics Act" as well as the "New Math" reforms since both opposing educational aims attempted to provide students with pedagogical techniques and curricula enhancements that would facilitate a high level of understanding of mathematics. The difference between these two reform packages may be their conceptions of mathematics, as well as the pedagogies they employed. For instance, in the Back to Basics reforms, absolutist conception of mathematics was more prevalent as well as traditional pedagogical approaches. In the "New Math" reform, the aesthetic conception of mathematics could be seen, as well as certain constructivist and political pedagogies utilized. Interestingly, one can also see the correlation between cognitive aims and constructivist strategies for learning with utilitarian aims of education. After all, public schooling in the United States at least was shaped by industrialists, notably Carnegie, Morgan, Rockfeller, and Ford in order to produce a docile and efficient workforce (Greer and Mukhopadhyay, 2003). Indeed, knowledge, either perceived as socially agreed upon or existing in a platonic realm, makes no difference in the ends such knowledge ought to be used for.

Democratic aims are the most difficult to pin down, since as we explained in Chapter 2 (p. 19), the policy in the United States tends to evoke democratic objectives as part of the overall discourse (Stone, 2002). For example, the infamous No Child Left Behind Act at least rhetorically claims to work towards this end. In regard to conception of mathematics, it would seem fallibilist claims seem to relate most easily to this objective since the cultural status of numbers would help loosen the western hegemonic power of mathematics. Certainly, the political pedagogies seem to correlate the easiest with democratic aims; however, all these depend on what definition of democracy one is using.

It would seem that utilitarian and democratic aims for mathematics education are the antithesis to each other, but this may not be the case. Indeed, in the current policy discourse, these two are completely intertwined. Similar to Steen's argument for mathematics literacy in a technological world, mathematics education is believed to be primarily for gaining the knowledge of mathematics that can best serve an individual living in the United States. If one believes that the United States is a functioning democracy, then it would be perfectly reasonable to use the meritocracy argument that mathematics education ought to aim to provide the knowledge and skill set needed to earn a living wage. On the other hand, if one is a critical pedagogue as Ernest's public educator aim depicts, democratic aims of mathematics education assume a much different agenda.

Not only has mathematics knowledge had ethical consequences; it can also be used for political possibilities. The connection between politics and ethics is essentially tied to the ideology behind democracy. Gutstein (2006) asserts that mathematics ought to be used for radically new democratic agendas, which can raise consciousness about the unjust practices of society. Thus, the philosophical domain of ethics seems to be the strongest link since it ties epistemology and political concerns of mathematics education together. Moreover, ethical inquiry may be better able to bridge the gap between epistemology and ontology. Political questions assume a particular stance on epistemology and thereby ontology. Ethical questions assume slightly less and therefore begin more at an opening of inquiry. Ethics also asks us to conceive of alternative possibilities; these possibilities may also stem from our misrepresentations of the world and the things within them. Hence, thinking about ontology can add a useful reflection to ethical questions.

Moving to science, we here review in more detail advanced scholarship in science education that fully critiques science education's axiological underpinnings. Pierce (2012) describes it as follows:

> "The connection between human capital and biocapitalism is particularly important to map since the human capital understanding of education is

foundational to the science education reform movement that is oriented toward a coproductive relationship between scientific literacy and biocapitalist economic imperatives. The concept of scientific literacy as it is operationalized in the current neo-Sputnik movement, in other words, cannot be understood outside the emergent regime of biocapitalism and the forms of subjectivities needed for its promissory futures to be realized." (p. 723)

In using the concept of biocapitalism, Pierce is drawing on the Foucauldian notion of biopower in which nation states regulate and control subjects through various mechanisms that subjugate individuals and their bodies. In this case the powerful transcends the nation state and is in actuality the global economic and political elite, transnational corporations and the like, who subjugate people as wage laborers. Science education's role in this, then, is seen as investment in which children, youth and adults are inculcated with skills and habits of mind from which the powerful can profit. As with mathematics education, the dominant value of science education is corporate control and profit. It is noted that corporate profit historically accompanies environmental degradation and social injustice.

Again, as with mathematics education, many have developed science educations with alternative values. As noted in the previous section, for years many have worked on STS and SSI and these are starting points. However, more assertive alternatives include the work of Roth and Barton (2004) and Hodson (2004). In *Rethinking Scientific Literacy*, Roth and Barton (2004) specifically question the values underlying mainstream science education. Their alternative centers on the notion of "citizen science," something

> "related to a variety of contexts, ranging from personal matters (e.g., accessibility to safe drinking water), livelihood (e.g., best farming practices), leisure (e.g., gardening in sustainable, organic ways), to activism or organized protest. In the community, however, citizen knowledge is collective and distributed: our lives in society are fundamentally based on the division of labor. If we need advice for a backache, we go to the doctor or chiropractor; if our cars or bicycles do not work, we go to the car or bicycle shop. In the same way, science in the community is distributed; scientific literacy in everyday community life means to be competent in finding whatever one needs to know at the moment one needs to know it." (p. 10)

This is clearly a science education that values democratic practice at the expense of corporate profit.

Hodson (2004) presents a four level process for scientific literacy that ultimately calls students to take action:

Level 1: Appreciating the societal impact of scientific and technological change, and recognizing that science and technology are, to some extent, culturally determined.

Level 2: Recognizing that decisions about scientific and technological development are taken in pursuit of particular interests, and that benefits accruing to some may be at the expense of others. Recognizing that scientific and technological developments are inextricably linked with the distribution of wealth and power.

Level 3: Developing one's own views and establishing one's own underlying value positions.

Level 4: Preparing for, and taking, action. (p. 3)

The values of Hodson's vision for science education are for increasing individual and community power so that, increasingly, democratic decision-making is at the core of social life, and when this mechanism fails, individuals and communities are empowered to take action.

Technology and engineering, although a bit more difficult to disentangle using philosophical constructs, has a huge role to play in the way in which STEM education reframes the goals and interests of our society. Postman has argued vehemently against education's love affair with all things technology. Although he has not specifically discussed STEM, we imagine his critique would be even harsher. He writes:

> "there is a kind of forthright determinism about the imagined world described in it. The technology is here or will be, we must use it because it is there, we will become the kind of people the technology requires us to be and, whether we like it or not, we will remake our institutions to accommodate the technology." (p. 39) End of Education

Postman warns us that for every advantage technology brings, there is also a disadvantage inherent in it (p. 192).

Upon reviewing philosophical inquiries of STEM education policies, we see a consistent theme in which human capital development is the kernel value for each. In other words, in this historical moment of the clear unification of STEM, our axiological analysis contends that STEM education is primarily for the benefit of global political and economic elites aiming to regulate bodies by investments and profit returns. In reviewing alternative values for mathematics and science education, we also suggest the possibilities for an alternative STEM value, rooted primarily in transformative education working towards democratic ideals.

Note

1. This debate rages forward through consructivist theories on learning mathematics, various schools in philosophy of mathematics, and poststructuralist critiques.

3
Critical Inquiry into STEM Education

Abstract: *In this chapter, we offer a detailed, rigorous inquiry into STEM education policy that uses philosophical methods resting primarily on the philosophical categories: axiology, ontology, and epistemology. In a deep exploration of the what, why, and how of STEM, we employ a unique approach rooted in the work of philosopher Alain Badiou. To begin, we review his writings on mathematics and set theory in particular, as this will launch our exploration. After which, we detail our approach in selecting and analyzing STEM policy documents. The inquiry and analysis reveal the revolutionary potential in STEM education, something that might not be intended by policy but exists nonetheless.*

Keywords: Alain Badiou; ontology; philosophical method; set theory

Chesky, Nataly Z. and Mark R. Wolfmeyer. *Philosophy of STEM Education: A Critical Investigation.* New York: Palgrave Macmillan, 2015. DOI: 10.1057/9781137535467.0008.

In this chapter, we offer a detailed, rigorous inquiry into STEM education policy that uses philosophical methods resting primarily on the philosophical categories introduced and discussed in the previous two chapters: axiology, ontology, and epistemology. In a deep exploration of the what, why, and how of STEM, we employ a unique approach rooted in the work of philosopher Alain Badiou. To begin, we review his writings on mathematics and set theory in particular, as this will launch our exploration. After which, we detail our approach in selecting and analyzing STEM policy documents. This reveals the revolutionary potential in STEM education, something that might not be intended by the policy but exists nonetheless. Such potentiality sets us up for the final chapter in which we detail an alternative STEM education.

3.1 Alain Badiou

A contemporary French philosopher writing today, Alain Badiou provides work that is highly useful for understanding the political climate in education, especially in STEM. Badiou's corpus is enormous and is only beginning to gain momentum in influencing the English-speaking philosophical community. As his many volumes of books and essays get translated into English, Badiou's unique philosophical pose and theoretical thought continue to stimulate modern philosophers working in various fields, one of which is philosophy of education (e.g., 2003, 2005a, 2005b, 2006, 2008). His work is most recently being utilized in theorizing revolutionary ideas in education (e.g., Barbour, 2010; Brown, 2010; Clemens, 2001; den Heyer, 2009; Hallward, 2006; Lehman, 2010; Lewis and Cho, 2005).

Badiou's work is particularly well suited to STEM policy analysis; first for the attention he gives to mathematics. One of Badiou's most famous statements is that "mathematics is ontology," or more specifically, mathematics is the only discourse that can think ontologically (Badiou, 2005a). In this section, we review what Badiou means by this, focusing on his assertion of being as a multiplicity. This leads to studying the nature of things, as Badiou argues via set theory. Taken as a whole, these considerations set forth the important role that mathematics, and thereby STEM, education can play in transforming society. In particular, this involves re-framing mathematical thought towards aesthetics. This section largely deals with mathematics and not the other content areas of

STEM. Although it has been suggested that mathematics is the backbone of STEM, we are careful not to adopt that concept here. Rather, Badiou's attention to mathematics can shift our thinking about mathematics and, in turn, STEM in its entirety.

Ontology, as defined by Badiou, is "a world" or "a situation" or more simply, it is what is presented in the world. His ontological axioms begin with a proclamation that "an objective situation in which subjective truths are at work is never anything other than a multiple, made up of an infinity of elements, which are themselves multiples" (2005a, p. 65). His ontology of the multiple directly opposes traditional Hegelian and classical Platonic views of unity and oneness, which posit that there is some causal determinate that necessarily exists before all else comes into being or that exists beyond in the realm of forms that gives essential structure to the world around us. For Badiou, the multiple is an ontological truth, and a method for understanding its relation to the world around us is axiomatic set theory, a branch of modern mathematics.

Set theory enables mathematicians to study sets, defined as a collection of objects, typically conceived of as mathematical entities, but also could be more simplistically defined as groups of any objects, such as people, and pencils; for example, a set can be a collection of objects on your desk, which at this moment happen to be a lamp, pencil, phone, and computer. Thus, the set of objects on your desk (at this particular time and place) are a lamp, a pencil, a phone, and a computer. A more mathematical example of a set is the set of all factors of the number 12, which are 12, 1, 2, 6, 3, and 4.

The contention that reality consists solely of multiplicity is a philosophical position that Badiou holds, which brings him to the conclusion that the language of set theory allows for multiplicity to be explored, since it only posits elements that can be themselves sets of sets. In mathematics, being can be thought, but perhaps not known completely insofar as mathematics is a meta-discourse that, while speaking about being, it has no means for deciphering it. Mathematicians therefore use the language of being in their proofs and theorems, but never gain the ability to fully understand the meaning of the mathematical language that they themselves utilize. Influenced by Russell, Badiou explains,

> Mathematics is a discourse in which one does not know what one is talking about nor whether what one is saying is true. Mathematics is rather the *sole* discourse, which "knows" absolutely what it is talking about. (2008, p. 8)

The reason for this, according to Badiou, is that mathematicians are interested in gaining knowledge, not uncovering truths.

An important distinction for Badiou is that truth is not equivalent to knowledge. In Badiou's framework truth is subtracted from knowledge just as being is subtracted from the void, which is defined as "something that exceeds the recognized differences in any given situation" (2005a, in Barbour, 2010, p. 255). The distinction between knowledge and truth is strikingly different from the current philosophical tradition, which claims only epistemic knowledge can be known and truth is only relative to the cultural paradigm from which it emerges. Badiou states that there are only four possible discrete conditions for truth to be produced (events); and it is within this discourse that Badiou sees the possibility to think the infinite, which in his conception is multiplicity or a multiple within multiple. This is why he insists that mathematics (particularly set theory) is the language of ontology, because it is the only language that can depict the multiple of things directly. Since being is pure multiplicity in Badiou's framework, mathematics, particularly set theory, is the rightful discourse to capture being at its essence.

In a twist on traditional Platonic disposition, Badiou does not believe mathematics has any objects, but rather, mathematics is a discourse. "Math is not a game without object, but a discourse of ontology" (2008, p. 5). Of course, this does not help us understand what constitutes ontology and its role in the situation. Badiou defines ontology as an "unfinished science trying to organize the discourse of presentation" (2005a, p. 8). This is true because ontology is not being but merely attempts to organize it. Being, cannot be known, it can only be "satured from the void" (ibid., p. 10). If mathematics is ontology, then a philosophy that studies mathematics is akin to meta-ontology since it only presents itself and not being; however, through its discourse we may come to understand where and how the *void* might emerge and therefore where *truth events* may occur and how *subjects* are created by their fidelity to these events. These are technical terms that mean specific things and are well defined by Badiou. As we progress through this chapter Badiou's terminology will be explained in detail.

If, according to Badiou, multiplicity is all that exists, the modern way of understanding numbers as discrete quantities is false. Yet, this pure "inconsistent multiple" is unthinkable and can only be represented as a "consistent multiple," which only occurs by an operation, Badiou terms the "count-as-one" that renders multiplicities measureable and perceptible (2005a). However, according to Badiou, the pure multiple can be retroactively understood by using the Zermolo Frankel axiomatic set theory. This is because utilizing a formal mathematics language such as set theory, one does not need to define the tools which one is using, only considering how well formed they are. Set theory allows the multiple to be thought since it does not try to understand the single entity of number, but is only interested in relationships or structures that numbers belong to. This interest in structures and relationships can be characterized, at least in our framework here, as an aesthetic ontological category. Resnik's (1981) definition of mathematics as a study of patterns and Shapiro's (1997) emphasis on structures in mathematics uphold the ontology of the multiple a Badiou has defined. Numbers in an aesthetic ontological view are conceptualized as only real insofar as they relate to one another, in a non-hierarchical structure. Thus, unlike the ontologists who came before him, Badiou asserts that unity does not exist, but only multiplicity. As with numbers, a number cannot exist without the set to which it belongs to. For example, the real number 4 is in the set of integers, which is itself a subset of rational numbers, which in turn is a subset of all real numbers, and so on. This ontological category provides a different ontology for thinking about how mathematics is conceived and therefore has implications for education and its policy reform discourses, in particular STEM, which is heavily supported and assessed by quantitative rationales. Understanding numbers as relations necessitates a pedagogical method that is more holistic and perhaps more cognitively intensive. Moreover, viewing numbers as relations changes the way in which they are utilized in standardized tests and other quantitative means for assessment of teachers and students since quantifiable results must be measured only in terms of them and not presented as static objective truths.

Galileo once said that the world "is written in the language of mathematics" (den Heyer, 2009, p. 233). Badiou agrees, and believes strongly that the present world adheres to a classical schema, which through the centuries has given humankind the tools and methods for learning about the reality in which we live. After all, without mathematics very little of humankind's accomplishments, such as skyscrapers and medical breakthroughs, and travesties, like the nuclear bomb, could have been achieved much less imagined. Technological advances from computers to all forms of digital devices rely on mathematical knowledge. Indeed, many involved in STEM education find mathematics to be its backbone.

Number, an ontological entity for Badiou, is not an objective measurement device, rather it is "a form of being" and our incessant propensity to control and manipulate "Number" has led to a collective amnesia that is the cause and effect of our human condition. Badiou writes:

> In our situation, that of Capital, the reign of number is thus the reign of the unthought slavery of numericality itself. Number, which so it is claimed, underlies everything of value, is in actual fact a proscription against any thinking of number itself. Number operates as that obscure point where the situation concentrates its law; obscures through its being at once sovereign and subtracted from all thought, and even from every investigation that orients itself towards a truth. (2008, p. 213)

Thus, if we seek a new definition of number, an alternative conception of mathematics, and a new method for teaching it, certain societal norms and values may change as well. For example, we would no longer value economic status as depicted by our bank accounts and earning statements to justify our worth; instead we may value how close our friendships and relationships are and what positive influences we have made. Simply, this is a question of how we come to perceive reality, as either quantifiable discrete parts or as relational interconnected points.

Badiou, like many European philosophers that came before him, is interested in political and social revolution. For Badiou, there are four places for newness to occur (politics, science, love, and art). These truth events happen at a point at the edge of the void, which is defined as the space in which what is presented in a situation suddenly appears to some subject who becomes aware of its presence yet knows that this variable was never represented in a normal situation. In mathematics education, this void can be found in situations where we become aware of the ontological status of mathematics. According to Badiou, the void can only occur within particular contextual situations, which are always subjective in interpretation; yet, although they are universal in the sense that everyone can be privy to them, one cannot name the specific conditions by which such situations arise, nor can one generalize anything about them.

Aesthetics in mathematics, at least in the way we are utilizing it here, is about ontology; thus conceptualizing numbers and other mathematical entities as relationships is an ontological category that stands as an alternative to the absolutist and fallibilistic ontological perspective. Badiou in *The Handbook of Inaesthetics* (2005b) theorizes the connection between art, philosophy, and education. He writes, "the norm of art must be education, and the norm of education is philosophy" (p. 3). Further, "art itself that educates because it teaches of the power of infinity held within the tormented cohesion of a form" (ibid., p. 3). As Badiou explains, the link between art and philosophy is education; therefore it may be through education that aesthetics can be conceptualized in terms of mathematics. "Inaeshetic education aims to loosen the hold of sensibility on the minds of the populace, and ideally, to corrupt the youth" (Lehman, 2010, p. 177). Since both art and science are sites for truths to emerge, it is absolutely imperative for educators and philosophers to take notice. This might be especially true for mathematics since more and more art programs are being removed from the public school curriculum. While mathematics education cannot substitute for the aesthetic experiences students learn in a pure art class, it can however infuse art within its structure. Perhaps, as many have argued (Dehaene, 1997; Devlin, 2000; Sinclair, N., Pimm, and Higginson, 2006), this combination will help students learn high level mathematics more effectively.

Philosophy's role is akin to meta-education or perhaps policy critique, since it arranges and exposes truths and attempts to disseminate them to a universal address. Badiou's method of set theoretical analysis can assist theorists and educators to make sense of policies at a more philosophical level.

3.2 Badiou's philosophical method: an example

Incorporating Alain Badiou's set theory method of analysis, this section examines the STEM discourse to understand the complex web that interconnects its inherent subject matter, pedagogy, and purpose (ontology, epistemology, and axiology). The method fuses mathematical language and method with Badiou's method of educational analysis to further complicate and understand STEM as the world's power elite has produced it. This reveals their mainstream efforts as well as promising spaces, or voids, in which transformative education can occur.

For this part of the book we were specifically interested in collecting publically accessible documents either explicitly from the US Department of Education or directly tied to them through funding or advocating activities, such as specific standardized test reports or particular policy recommendation reports. In order to capture these documents, we incorporated a recursive strategy for data collection.

More specifically, we began with a search in the ed.gov website for policy documents. After these were collected, we expanded the search using the Google search engine with the key words US education policy and mathematics. Next, we considered the National Council of Teachers of Mathematics (NCTM) website and National Science Foundation (NSF) for their policy recommendation documents.

Once we began coding, certain documents referenced others, hence the recursive nature of the document retrieval process. We found these documents that were referenced in others and included them if they met the criteria of being about mathematics generally, and public education in the United States particularly. As these documents were coded, we continuously did a Google search for others and looked in the ed.gov website for any new policy statements. The last several documents were found in research articles that referenced certain initiatives or funding agencies that were linked to the governmental policy programs. We retrieved the ones that were relevant within the research articles as well. We stopped the data collection process after we could not find any new documents that fit within our time frame. This means that we no longer found any documents that discussed anything new and we found similar coding practices throughout the documents. Once the pattern was repetitive and we gathered all the public documents that were referenced in journals, government websites, and NCTM and NSF literature, we knew it was time to finish the collecting process and begin the analysis. In total, we coded 38 documents, ranging in page length from about 10 to 200 pages.

Before explaining our analysis process, we would like to mention several important considerations about policy documents themselves. Policy documents are not static entities that exist outside the socio-political world out of which they arise. Rather, they are influenced by and created in socio-political contexts that are negotiated and agreed by the people within a society that hold a power position which enables them to disseminate their own values, norms, and beliefs onto the masses. "Documents often present and represent the committed positions of groups and individuals on policy issues and therefore can be analyzed to show how particular discourses are dominant, or where tensions in policy reflect struggles between various values" (Sharp and Richardson, 2001, p.199). Understanding policy documents is the way researchers can study the normative assumptions a particular society has on certain issues and disciplines. In the case of this study, views on what

STEM education ought to serve, how it ought to proceed, and what it ought to encompass are all societally held normative assumptions. These assumptions are found in policy documents, since these documents help shape and often reflect the norms held by groups that have the authoritative power to make decisions about what is best for citizens and their children when it comes to their education.

Extrapolating the norms a society has on a particular issue is a difficult undertaking. However, analysis of public policy documents provides a method by which researchers can view the rhetoric and discourse surrounding highly political societal issues of great importance, such as STEM education in the 21st century. Marshall and Rossman (1999) explain that the review of documents is an "unobtrusive method, rich in portraying the values and beliefs of participants in the setting" (p. 116). In other words, documents can be seen as social texts, which "emerge out of, but also produce, particular policy discourses" (Jackmore and Lander 2005, p. 100). Analysis of policy documents has the potential to expand the research done in policy studies beyond simple implementation advocacy or critique, but to broader areas of discussion about the very purposes of educational policy and how or why such purposes can be used.

The methodology we used initially is content analysis, which could be classified as a mixed method approach. Later, we supplemented content analysis with Badiou's methodology of using set theory. Next, we first discuss the content analysis approach, which comprised most of the coding process and then we explain the addition of the set theory approach, which occurred at the end of our analysis of the data.

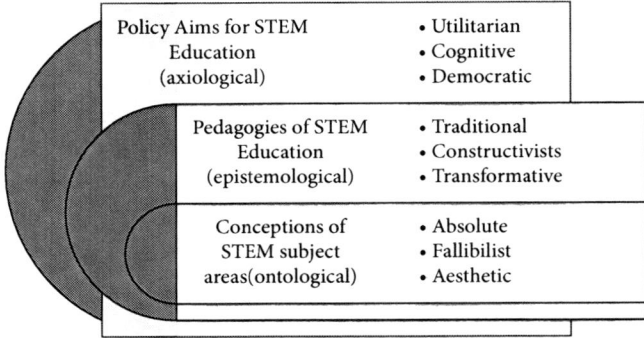

FIGURE 3.1 *Analytic constructs for coding*

We used both qualitative and quantitative strategies in the study, since we were interested in understanding not only the relationship of claims and assumptions about STEM content and its education found in policy text but we were also interested in gathering numeric frequency of the appearance of these categories. We believe that each type of finding, numerical frequency of categories, and a qualitative analysis of how these categories fit within the larger structure of the discourse, complements the other. Qualitative content analysis encourages a deep familiarity with the documents, which can then lead to identification of key themes so as to draw inferences from the textual material (Perakyla, 2005). By gathering both quantitative and qualitative results, our analysis of the data was enriched.

Our original conviction before starting the analysis is that there should be cohesiveness to the way modern education conceptualizes STEM subjects, how it is taught, and for what primary purposes its education is believed to be for. From a decade of teaching and research experience in mathematics and science education, our intuition is that such cohesiveness is not present in the discourses surrounding both alternative approaches to STEM education and in dominant views as expressed in national policy documents about STEM education. However, after completing the study, we found that cohesiveness is more complex than we had originally speculated in policy reform texts. As the findings section will explain, the lack of cohesiveness may not be a detriment to policy reform discourses. In fact, the lack of cohesiveness may not be a drawback at all, but rather, it may open the space for the potential for positive consequences for teachers and STEM learners to explore. Even more radical, the incoherence present in the policy documents is instrumental to Badiou's revolutionary event insofar as multiplicity, which as truth of reality for Badiou, cannot be completely represented. Thus, there is always an incoherence to policies since they are by their very nature unable to capture the complexity of reality as such. Such lack of coherence, while viewed as a drawback by policy researchers, is for Badiou a wonderful consequence.

The coding process was a threefold process. To begin, we coded each document for particular phrases that met the analytic constructs we delegated and justified as important. These are explained thoroughly in Chapter 2 of this book. The categories were axiology, epistemology, and ontology. The codes were originally generated by our in-depth study of STEM education, philosophy of STEM subjects, and philosophy of education.

The second round of coding paid specific attention to word choice and grammatical usage. We found certain words/phrases repeated in the documents and counted these words within the subcategories. The particular words we were interested in coding for arose organically through a grounded approach as depicted by Krippendorff (2004). At this time, we speculated that the key words and/or phrases would range from the following three categories with the possible words:

Category	Word/phrase
Ontological	Reality, social, practical, beautiful, organic, faulty, cultural
Epistemological	Construct, memorize, drill, invent, discover, meaningful
Axiological	Competition, technology, literate, aesthetic, skills

In addition to coding each document for the nine different categories (the three main categories with three subcategories each), we recorded words and/or phrases that seemed to recur often. A simple tally system using paper and pencil was on hand during the computerized coding process. In this way, we were able to keep track of words and phrases that we noticed often and their frequency. Once the coding procedure was completed, we went back to the tally sheet and reviewed the ten most recurring words/phrases. Then we repeated the tally using the computer's "finder" function for the folder that contained all the documents. We recorded this number as well as two examples each of the context in which the words/phrases appeared.

The third round of coding aimed at understanding the relationships between subcategories, as they existed within each policy document. We used tables and an experimental methodology of mathematics axiomatic set theory to understand the relationship among the three research categories. Here, a simplistic version of set theory, which only utilizes some basic language and operations, was used to try and theorize where a Badiouian event might occur, or for Badiou's concerns, where the void in policy documents exists, since that is precisely where an event has the potentiality to be found or witnessed by a subject.

3.3 Research findings

This section offers detailed descriptive findings from the empirical content analysis study conducted for this book. The findings are presented amongst four tables, each exhibiting in a different way how we made sense of the data. We offer extensive mathematical analysis not because we feel it is valid and objective, but to offer a rich description of the data so that the reader, as well as the researcher, can interpret the findings in a thoughtful, knowledgeable way. The first section (A) gives an overall picture of the findings by using tables and graphs. The second section (B) offers more detailed examples of the words and/or phrases that most commonly appear in the documents. Section C delves further into the interrelations of the codes and how they appear in each document. Lastly, Section D is the experimental Badiouian set theory method that strives to understand what elements are present in the policy documents but not included.

The total data points (policy documents) that completed the survey of available public documents about US STEM education were 38. After completing the coding process, the study yielded a total of 1123 codes. As expected, the codes in the axiological category were most prevalent. This outcome was expected because we were dealing with policy documents, which are inherently about prescribing objectives education ought to meet. While all three subcategories of axiology had a large presence in the coding, the utilitarian axiological claim was most prevalent with 240 coding instances. Very closely behind was the democratic axiological category, with a total of 209 instances in the documents. The cognitive axiological claim came up 136 times. However, axiology was not the most prevalent of the codes present in the documents since the epistemological code for traditional came up 259 times, beating the most popular code. The next most popular epistemological class was constructivist with 116 coding instances, followed by transformative with only 12 coding instances. As for the ontological codes, these came up relatively less than the other categories, but this was expected due to the nature of rhetoric in policy documents. The code for absolutist came up 87 times, which is comparable with the axiological category of cognitive (136 instances) and the epistemological category of constructivists (116 instances). Interestingly, the aesthetic ontological category showed up 57 times in the documents and the fallibilistic category in ontology only came up seven times. Although all the codes had a minimum of zero, which means that there was at least one document in the data set that did not include any given code, they all had different maximum values, which specify the maximum amount of times a code appeared in the data set. Table 3.1 presents a bar graph depicting the overall distribution of the codes in the policy documents.

TABLE 3.1 *Total coding distribution*

Code	Total	Min	Max	Mean	Std. Dev.
Axiology—Cognitive (AC)	136	0	136	34	61.514
Axiology—Democratic (AD)	209	0	209	52.25	100.54
Axiology—Utilitarian (AU)	240	0	240	60	120
Epistemology—Constructivist (EC)	116	0	116	29	58
Epistemology—Traditional (ET)	259	0	259	64.75	128.834
Epistemology—Transformative (EF)	12	0	12	3	6
Ontology—Absolutist (OA)	87	0	87	21.75	43.5
Ontology—Aesthetic (OE)	57	0	57	14.25	28.5
Ontology—Fallibilistic (OF)	7	0	7	1.75	3.5

At first glance it seems that the two most prominent categories were ET and AU. However, when combining the subcategories, we get axiology totaling 585 and epistemology with 387 codes. This makes the highest code of ET even more apparent and the axiology code utilitarian less so, since relatively speaking the utilitarian code did not add the majority of codes to the axiology category but was mixed with the democratic and cognitive codes. The epistemology codes for constructivist (116) and transformative (12) did not make as much of a contribution to the overall epistemology coding category. However, it is interesting to note that the code for EC, 116, did appear slightly less than the code for AC, 136. The axiology codes of democracy and utilitarian were relatively strong since the former had 52 as a mean and the latter had 60.

The epistemology codes took up a large percentage of the total codes, perhaps more than expected, since policies are mostly written for overall objectives they wish to achieve. Not surprisingly, the traditional epistemology category dominated, with a mean of 64.75. Next was the constructivist category, which had a 29 mean code frequency. Last, the transformative epistemology category only had an average of 3. These are not surprising findings since the literature on STEM education policy dictated that standardization, content knowledge, and expertise were essential to knowledge and ought to influence the way in which STEM education is taught in the United States.

The occurrence of ontological codes was relatively small in comparison to the other coding categories, but again this is to be expected. However, it was still encouraging to find ontological reference in the policy discourse. We were surprised to find very few codes for fallibilist ontological category and as much aesthetic codes as we found in the documents. Even though the absolutist subcategory was predominant at 87 codes, the aesthetic subcategory did fare comparably at 57 total codes. The average of these two codes is even more similar with the former scoring 21.75 as a mean and the latter 14.25.

Figures 3.2 and 3.3 give a visual display of the distribution of codes in the policy documents.

The bar graph in Figure 3.2 shows the frequency of codes in relation to one another and the pie graph depicts the percentages of average codes

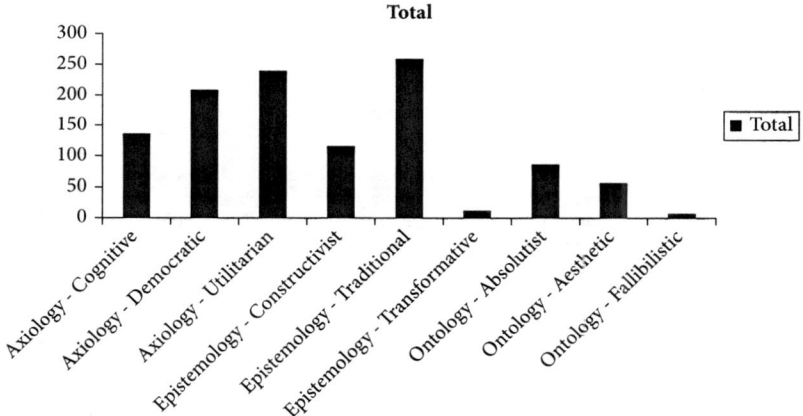

FIGURE 3.2   *Comparison of total codes*

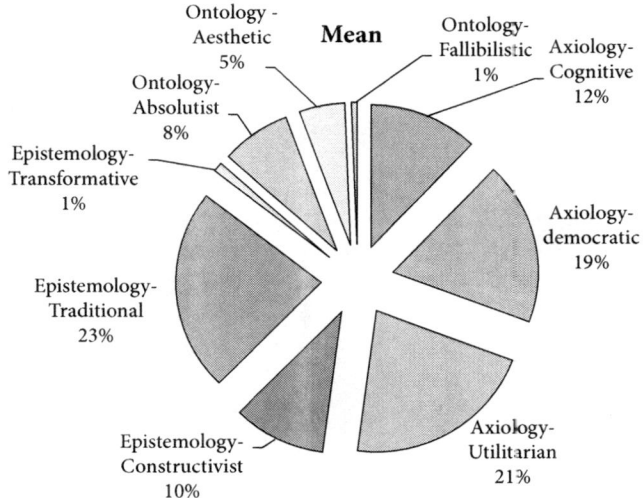

FIGURE 3.3   *Comparison of average distribution of codes*

DOI: 10.1057/9781137535467.0008

in relation to the total codes present in the documents. The epistemology category of transformative is similar to the ontological category of fallibilistic, both at 1% of the total codes given. The two ontological categories of absolutism and aesthetic are similar in comparison to the remaining coding categories. The epistemological category of constructivism at 10% of the codes is similar to the axiological category of cognitive, which is 12% of the total codes. The remaining, more dominant categories have relatively equal coding percentages, at 21% which is AU, 23% for ET, and 19% for AD.

TABLE 3.2 *Distribution of codes per document*

Document Name	Axiological			Epistemological			Ontological			Total in Document
	AU	AC	AD	ET	EC	EF	OA	OF	OE	
21st Century Community Learning Centers	0	2	2	0	0	0	0	0	0	4
Blueprint for Reform	5	6	28	5	0	1	0	0	0	45
Achieving the Common Core	0	7	1	1	0	0	1	0	1	11
Adding It Up	5	1	5	5	8	0	5	3	2	34
America Competes Act	7	6	4	4	0	0	0	0	0	21
American Competitiveness Initiative	16	5	10	14	0	1	0	0	0	46
An International Perspective on Mathematics	1	2	2	2	2	1	1	1	3	15
A Parent Guide: Multiply Your Child's Success	2	1	0	1	0	0	0	0	2	6
Before It's Too Late	13	3	7	5	3	0	4	0	0	35
Coordinating Federal State Policy	13	3	13	1	0	0	0	0	0	30
Counting on Excellence	4	3	2	2	0	0	1	0	0	12
CRS Report 2006	2	0	3	1	1	0	0	0	0	7

Continued

TABLE 3.2 Continued

Document Name	Axiological			Epistemological			Ontological			Total in Document
	AU	AC	AD	ET	EC	EF	OA	OF	OE	
CRS Report 2008	2	0	0	0	0	0	0	0	0	2
Common Core Standards	0	11	0	46	46	0	42	0	31	176
Curriculum and Evaluation Standards (NCTM)	2	6	7	2	12	4	0	0	4	37
Defining a 21st Century Education	9	7	0	2	0	0	2	0	5	25
Education and the American Jobs Act	4	1	1	0	0	0	0	0	0	6
Everybody Counts	1	3	7	1	6	3	1	1	1	24
Executive Summary: Principles and Standards for School Mathematics (NCTM)	3	3	0	0	2	0	0	0	2	10
Gender Differences	0	0	3	0	0	0	0	0	0	3
Highlights from PISA Results	1	1	0	0	0	1	0	0	0	3
Math Teachers: The Nation Builders of the 21st century	9	6	3	2	0	0	1	0	0	21
Mathematics and Science Partnerships	3	4	4	10	20		3	1	1	46
NCLB a Desktop Reference	0	2	5	7	0	0	0	0	0	14
NCLB Math and Science Partnership Part B	0	2	0	2	0	0	0	0	0	4
NMSI 2011 Annual Report	10	6	7	3	0	1	0	0	0	27

Continued

TABLE 3.2　*Continued*

	Axiological			Epistemological			Ontological			Total in Document
Document Name	AU	AC	AD	ET	EC	EF	OA	OF	OE	
Race to the Top Program Executive Summary	2	9	19	9	0	0	0	0	0	39
Report to the President Prepare and Inspire	5	1	4	2	1	0	0	0	1	14
Rising Above the Gathering Storm	6	0	0	0	0	0	0	0	0	6
Science and Mathematics Education Policy White Paper	3	2	3	13	4	1	3	0	0	29
Science and Mathematics: A Formula for 21st Century Success	19	9	13	18	0	0	0	0	0	59
STEM Education: A Primer	2	0	4	0	0	0	0	0	0	6
Supporting STEM	21	3	4	5	1	9	3	0	0	46
The Federal STEM Education Portfolio	6	1	7	3	1	0	0	0	0	18
The Final Report National Advisory Report	12	0	4	24	0	0	10	0	0	50
The US Science and Technology Workforce	10	0	2	0	0	0	0	0	0	12
Tapping America's Potential	12	1	2	7	1	0	0	0	0	23
Uteach Brochure	3	0	2	2	3	0	0	0	2	12

Table 3.2 depicts a detailed look into each policy document and the codes found in them. The documents are listed and each main category (axiology, epistemology, and ontology) is broken up into their subcategories. The numbers in each column stand for the number of times each particular code appeared in each particular document. For example, the code for AC appeared in the 21st century community centers two times. The final column shows the total number of codes found in each document.

The first thing we notice from this table is that very few of the documents had the fallibilistic ontological claim or the transformative epistemological assertion. On the contrary, most documents had the three axiological claims together and many had both traditional and constructivist epistemologies present. To offer a concise picture of the policy documents, the analysis shows fairly equally democratic and utilitarian axiological claims and traditional and constructivist epistemological assertions. In addition, both the absolutist and aesthetic ontological assumptions were evident and seemed to be dispersed equally among the axiological assertions.

Next, we extrapolate a method, used by Badiou for understanding where a radical change can occur in the political sphere, to understand where transformative change may occur in the educational sphere. The purpose of this method is to provide a philosophical perspective for educational researchers, and especially for educators themselves, to utilize in their own practice so that they (1) have a more clear sense of the policies that shape their classrooms and (2) develop a sense of agency in enacting pedagogical techniques that leave space for the possibility for truth events to occur within the classroom.

Before developing this methodology, several explanations must take precedence. They are Badiou's system for classifying presentation/representation, his foundational axioms of which he gives no proof, and his description of truth procedures. To explain how we used Badiou's philosophical method in this final section, we first need to showcase the uniqueness of his method. Unlike Dewey's synthesis or a Hegelian triadic, Badiou sees reality as always a state within a state or a reality within a reality. The table below better explains this:

Situation	State of the situation
Presented	Represented
Belonging	Including
Count-as-one	Second count

The situation is what exists in our world and the state of the situation is how we understand it or come to represent it: "A situation in which at least one multiple on the edge of the void is presented" (2005a, p 75). Since in Badiou's ontology there are only multiples and the one is not, we begin with presentation as a count, which makes the infinite pure multiple comprehensible to us. This multiple is said to belong to the situation and be presented. The second count is akin to our reflection about the situation, and this is where the multiple (which is not quantifiable) is counted again and represented as included in the situation. An example of this is a citizen who belongs to the United States by birth, is counted in the census for population demographic purposes, yet does not vote or hold any public office or engage in any public activities whatsoever. The citizen can be included and represented if he does vote and/or runs for mayor of his small town, for instance. Within the situation's structure and the state of the situation's meta-structure, there always exists a void. This is not proved or justified by Badiou, since it is given as a prior as a characteristic of being itself, a concept of which we can have no knowledge of. What we must understand about the void, is like the mathematical concept of the null set, that it is inherent in all situations, universally included, and thereby, a subset of all other sets.

A site is the gathering of all non-presented elements of a situation, but it is the event that will determine if some subject, who remains faithful to it, gathered any elements. There are four kinds of sites in any given situation:

- Normal: presented and represented, include and belong
- Excrescence: represented but not presented, include but not belong
- Singular: presented but not represented, belong but not included
- Historical: at least one eventual site, at the edge of the void. (2005a, p. 188)

A Normal situation as defined by Badiou is the state of the situation. A historical situation is any situation in which newness or change occurs. This change can occur within any of the four truth conditions that Badiou categorized as happening in the realms of love, politics, mathematics, and art. Badiou's most popular examples are the Maoist revolution in China, or Marcel Duchamp's "fountain" that revolutionized what was considered art. In an excrescence situation something is included that does not belong, for example when votes are counted from noncitizens in a political race or poll or when demographics of a particular cultural group include another cultural group that does not affiliate itself with the first. Badiou does not spend too much time discussing this situation, and is much more interested

Critical Inquiry into STEM Education 63

in the singular situation, since for him this type of situation provides the necessary conditions for revolutionary change to occur. A singular situation occurs when something that belongs in the situation is not included or is presented but not represented in the final (second count). For example, when a particular demographic group of voters are included as citizens but not included in political polls. Another example is when a cultural group is included as industrial workers in a corporation, but their views and needs are not represented as part of the corporate world.

Badiou's agenda is to understand the conditions by which newness, or as he terms it, an event, takes place. These conditions happen with existing situations that structure our socio-political, cultural, and scientific worlds, as well as our personal loving relationships. Given Badiou's ontology of infinite multiplicity in any given presentation, it is impossible for everything to be represented that is presented or all things to be included that which belongs. Standardization wants to deny the multiplicity or the complexity of the situation. The claims, objectives, and perceptive formulas in policy documents are represented as the totality of the situation that is educational policy landscape in the United States today. However, there is much more information that is not represented but merely "belongs" within the situation. This minor discrepancy for Badiou would signify that there is a void to which a truth event can emerge.

By exploring the landscape of STEM policy discourse, we attempt to map the state of the situation. This method leaves the situation as such subjective only in the sense that it cannot be completely documented or represented through the policy documents that exist. However, by utilizing Badiou's method of set theory, researchers can investigate the reality that exists before the state of situation has had its "second count." What we will be looking for in this method is where there might be a Badiouian "void" that can only be found in a singular situation, defined as having at least one element that is presented but not represented, belong but not included. This element, in our analysis, must be a code that stands for either educational objectives (axiological), claims of knowledge (epistemology), or conceptions of mathematics and science (ontology).

What we must remember through the analysis of the findings is that there is an inherent paradox in policies, since they attempt to explain everything, and prescribe increasingly more detailed actions, curricula, and standards. But in its attempts to do so, it opens more of the void in that it becomes apparent to the policy analysis that there is indeed more complexity to be found and understood, and to the educator in the classroom it becomes apparent when they realize that no amount of planning, assessing, and prior experience, can prepare them for the particulars of the daily life in a classroom. In more Badiouian terms, in every attempt to be coherent, there is an incoherence produced by the void at the heart of the state.

Badiou framed his question this way: "The question is not whether possibilities are possible but is there the possibility for new possibilities?" The difference between these two options is critically important. In the first question—"Are possibilities possible?"—existing possibilities are found within the frame itself, while in the second—"Are new possibilities possible?"—a restructuring of the very frame of possibilities opens up beyond the closure of the present moment. Badiou's answer to this second question is an emphatic yes! Badiou's definition of a political activists is those who are "patient watchmen of the void instructed by the end" (2005a, p. 110).

In this section of the findings, we attempt a new methodology not used in policy analysis thus far: set theory. While the content analysis done in the previous section yielded a wealth of important information, it could not nearly give us a rich understanding of the philosophical assumptions and beliefs that are cogent within STEM policy discourse. Nor could it help us see what is the question that was anchored in our philosophical understanding of Badiou and what his theoretical lens could offer to STEM education. Therefore, our objective in doing this work is to find where what Badiou terms the void may be located in STEM education policy. In practical terms, our aim is to find where the coherence loses its structure in such a way that the discourse shows an anomaly that cannot be placed neatly within the overall discourse of STEM education policy. It is this void, or glitch if you will, that may be the deciding place for change for the researchers who critique STEM education policies, as well as a place of rich learning for educators to utilize in their everyday pedagogical and curricula decisions.

In what follows we attempt using the functions of set theory to see what coding categories become explicit in the documents and how such categories are related to one another. Badiou's definition of the "state of the situation" has been contextualized here to be US STEM education policy. What we are trying to understand is within this situation, what kinds of discourses are left presented but not represented, since this is precisely where Badiou believes is the potential for the void to emerge and new revolutionary truths to become known to a subject or subjects that witness and remain faithful to it.

In this methodology every element is also a set itself and each set can be an element of another set. For instance the set known as a particular policy document has the subcategories from our coding as elements, but these elements are also sets since they contain all particular instances (quotes) found in the policy documents. Our domain here is the set of policy documents that we have included in our analysis, which we explained in the methods chapter, were gathered by finding all the current nationally recognized US public educational policy documents that had a clear interest in mathematics education. While this may be interpreted as a closed set mathematically, we are well aware that new policy documents can be decided upon and then disseminated at any point during this process. However, this limitation does not hinder our analysis since the robust domain we have collected and are analyzing here contain a wide array of policy documents that we feel best exemplifies the "state of the situation." Another important note to take into account when performing mathematical set theory is that the amount of times an element exists in any given set is of no consequence and is only shown once in the written set. Thus, in this method we are not interested in frequency of how many times a particular code appeared in a document, but only that it appeared once. Below is a list all the policy documents and the elements they contain:

21st Century Community Learning Centers:	{AC, AD}
Blueprint for Reform:	{AU, AC, AD, ET, EF}
Achieving the Common Core:	{AC, AD, ET, CA, OE}
Adding It Up:	{AU, AC, AD, ET, EC, OA, OF, OE}
America Competes Reauthorization Act:	{AU, AC, AD, ET}
American Competitiveness Initiative:	{AU, AC, AD, ET, EF}
A Parent Guide:	{AU, AC, ET, OE}
Before It's Too Late:	{AU, AC, AD, ET, EC, OA}
Coordinating Federal STEM Policy:	{AU, AC, AD, ET}
Counting on Excellence:	{AU, AC, AD, ET, OA}
CRS Report STEM 2006:	{AU, AD, ET, EC}
CRS Report for Congress (2008):	{AU}
Common Core Standards:	{AC, ET, EC, OA, OE}
Curriculum and Evaluation Standards:	{AU, AC, AD, ET, EC, EF, OE}
Defining a 21st Century Education:	{AU, AC, ET, OA, OE}
Education and the American Jobs Act:	{AU, AC, AD}
Everybody Counts:	{AU, AC, AD, ET, EC, EF, OA, OF, OE}
Executive Summary NCTM:	{AU, AC, EC, OE}
Gender Differences:	{AD}
Highlights from PISA:	{AU, AC, EF}
An International Perspective:	{AU, AC, AD, ET, EC, EF, OA, OF, OE}
National Mathematics Advisory Panel:	{AU, AD, ET, OA}
Math Teachers:	{AU, AC, AD, ET, OA}
Mathematics and Science Partnerships:	{AU, AC, AD, ET, EC, OA, OF, OE}
NCLB: A Desktop Reference:	{AC, AD, ET}

NCLB Mathematics and Science Partnership:	{AC, ET}
NMSI 2011 Annual Report:	{AU, AC, AD, ET, EF}
Race to the Top Program:	{AU, AC, AD, ET}
Report to the President Prepare and Inspire:	{AU, AC, AD, ET, EC, OE}
Rising Above the Gathering Storm:	{AU}
Science and Mathematics:	{AU, AC, AD, ET}
Science and Mathematics Education Policy:	{AU, AC, AD, ET, EC, EF, OA}
STEM Education:	{AU, AD}
Supporting STEM:	{AU, AC, AD, ET, EC, EF, OA}
The Federal STEM Education Portfolio:	{AU, AC, AD, ET, EC}
The US Science and Technology Workforce:	{AU, AD}
Tapping America's Potential:	{AU, AC, AD, ET, EC}
UTeach Brochure:	{AU, AD, ET, EC, OE}

The code that appears in practically every policy document is AU, minus six documents, which means that AU was in 84% of the total policy documents. AC is missing in eight documents, which means AC was in 80% of the total policy documents. AD is missing in eight documents, the same as AC. ET is not in 10 articles a 26% discrepancy. This is an important finding since even though epistemology scored the highest overall coding frequency it was missing in more articles than the other popular codes. This means that although epistemology was discussed frequently in the policy documents, it was not discussed as much as other categories in all the policy documents combined. This makes sense given that some policy documents, like the Common Core or NCTM probably referenced epistemological claims often and many, but in other documents, ET was not mentioned at all. EC is missing in 18 articles, which means it did appear in 53% of the total policy documents.

The findings that are most interesting for this book are in the ontological category, since we contend that our ontological assumptions we hold about STEM content are essential to epistemological claims about how best to teach STEM and axiological objectives that specify the overall purposes STEM education ought to serve. Overall, the ontological category (all three subcategories of OA, OF, and OE) was missing in 20 of the 38 documents, which means that it was in 58% of the total documents. The code for OE played a more prominent role than we had anticipated in policy documents. Our assumption that it would not be very common in the policy documents stemmed originally from our review of policy discourse and the overwhelming support of utilitarian objectives and social constructivist epistemologies, neither of which did we originally believe correlated with an aesthetic ontological stance based on philosophical literature. The code of OA was not present in 26 of the documents and was present in 12. However, when accounted for only the documents that discussed ontology, which was 18 in total, OA occurred 67% of the time. OF occurred in four documents only, OE occurred in 12 documents and was not present in 26, the same as OA. This is an interesting finding to consider. We did not anticipate OE being as present in the policy documents as OA since our assumption was that traditional epistemologies would associate with an absolutist conception of STEM and utilitarian objectives would also not be interesting in an aesthetic way of viewing STEM. These incorrect assumptions we had about the way in which policy documents would correlate our three philosophical categories will be discussed in the next chapter. Thus, we believe the findings thus far give reason to explore the ontological category of aesthetics further, since our own assumptions as a professional educator and researcher caused us to be surprised about this finding. We believe many others in our position would also be surprised by this finding and therefore, we will investigate, using set theory, more closely the policy documents that have the category OE within them. The list of such policy documents is given below:

Achieving the Common Core:	{AC, AD, ET, OA, OE}
Adding It Up:	{AU, AC, AD, ET, EC, OA, OF, OE}
A Parent Guide:	{AU, AC, ET, OE}
Common Core Standards:	{AC, ET, EC, OA, OE}
Curriculum and Evaluation Standards:	{AU, AC, AD, ET, EC, EF, OE}
Defining a 21st Century Education:	{AU, AC, ET, OA, OE}
Everybody Counts:	{AU, AC, AD, ET, EC, EF, OA, OF, OE}
Executive Summary NCTM:	{AU, AC, EC, OE}
An International Perspective:	{AU, AC, AD, ET, EC, EF, OA, OF, OE}
Mathematics and Science Partnerships:	{AU, AC, AD, ET, EC, OA, OF, OE}
Report to the President Prepare and Inspire:	{AU, AC, AD, ET, EC, OE}
UTeach Brochure:	{AU, AD, ET, EC, OE}

What do all these documents have in common? The code for AU is found in all but two, and AC is found in all but one. We have a combination of ET and EC codes and a few fallibilistic ontology codes mixed in. Most predominant, though, are the links between OE and AC and AU. Also quite important to note is the lack of AD. Seven of them have the code OA included. There are 12 total documents with OE, and seven have OA as well, that is about half or to be more precise 58%. Given how pervasive the absolutist claim seems to be, this might be an important finding. Since many documents could not even be coded with an ontological category, understanding the frequency of this code is difficult to discern. Out of the 38 data points (policy documents), 18 had any code for ontology. Out of those 18, only six had codes for only absolutism and not aesthetic. This leaves 12 of the documents that had any code for ontology to have also aesthetics represented. We believe this is an important finding since aesthetic category is well presented in the policy discourse, although its representation (how many times it explicitly gets referenced) is relatively small. Relative to all the ontological codes, aesthetics had a stronger than expected showing, especially given the policy documents pertaining to utilitarian discourse.

With regard to the epistemology–ontology relationship, out of the 12 articles that had OE code present; 11 had ET as well. This means that one article did not have ET, but EC instead. We would imagine the EC code to appear more often with OE than ET since constructivist learning pedagogy often stresses the importance of eliciting wonder and excitement for the learner. However, sometimes child-centered approaches fail to do so, especially when they do not take into account the aesthetic component of mathematics. This is a critique of constructivism that was discussed at length in Chapter 2.

The above can only help us so far, which is again why we believe set theory can be a powerful methodology for our purposes here. Below, we conduct more set theoretical analysis using only the documents that have at least one code of OE. We begin by naming each document, alphabetically in bold, to better facilitate the set theory method. In this manner, a particular document is now defined as a set and the codes found within that document are elements in that set. They can also be "subsets" of a set if and only if all the elements included in one set are part of the larger set. For example, A is the set of codes found in achieving the common core. For example, the set of AC is the set of coding expressions found in policy documents about STEM education in the United States insofar as we have defined them in terms of a closed system of documents (the 38 we have collected as well as the coding scheme we developed utilizing the codebook and philosophical analytic constructs). Below, the first set is written in English as the set **A**, named Achieving the Common Core, and it has the elements AC, AD, ET, OA, and OE included with it. From now on when we use the bold capital "**A**," "**B**," "**C**," and so on, it stands for a particular policy document we have defined below:

A: Achieving the Common Core = {AC, AD, ET, OA, OE}
B: Adding It Up = {AU, AC, AD, ET, EC, OA, OF, OE}

C: A Parent Guide = {AU, AC, ET, OE}
D: Common Core Standards ={AC, ET, EC, OA, OE}
E: Curriculum and Evaluation Standards = {AU, AC, AD, ET, EC, EF, OE}
F: Defining a 21st Century Education = {AU, AC, ET, OA, OE}
G: Everybody Counts = {AU, AC, AD, ET, EC, EF, OA, OF, OE}
H: Executive Summary NCTM = {AU, AC, EC, OE}
I: An International Perspective = {AU, AC, AD, ET, EC, EF, OA, OF, OE}
J: Mathematics and Science Partnerships = {AU, AC, AD, ET, EC, OA, OF, OE}
K: Report to the President Prepare and Inspire = {AU, AC, AD, ET, EC, OE}
L: UTeach Brochure = {AU, AD, ET, EC, OE}

A technical note: The universal set always includes the null set, and every set above includes the null set as well. For Badiou, this is crucial since the null set is potentially where the void is located and thus all possibilities of events to materialize. However, in set theory as used in mathematics, the null set is trivial, since it is by definition included in every set. We have not visually represented it in our analysis here because although we are searching for the void, we take Badiou's assertion that the event occurs during a singularity. This singularity is when there is an element in the situation, which is represented but not presented. We interpreted this theoretical assertion in our empirical analysis as finding a code that stands out in some way beyond the representation of the codes in policy documents. Although we did not know what knowledge we would gain from doing set theoretical analysis on policy documents, we did so as a methodology and theoretical experiment. Regardless of this method's newness in analyzing policy documents, we utilized the formal conventions of set theory and as mathematicians often do say, the work if done systematically and following the rules of agreed upon mathematical operations, the findings often are a surprise.

First let us say a bit more about the new sets we have defined above, A through L and the operations of set theory we use to study them. A union is an operation in set theory that combines the elements in a group of sets. An intersection is an operation in set theory that only includes the elements found in all the sets that are grouped. For example, the set whose members are X and Y is written: {X,Y}. The union of sets X and Y denotes the set of all elements in either X or Y (or both), written: {X∪Y}. If set X has the elements 1, 2, 3 and set Y has the elements 3, 4, then the union would be the set of elements 1, 2, 3, 4. This is written as {X∪Y} = {1, 2, 3, 4}. The intersection of sets X and Y denotes the set of elements that are in both X and Y, written: {X∩Y}. Again, taking the example just posed above, the intersection of sets X and Y would be the set of element 3. This is written as {X∩Y} = {3}. Sets X and Y are said to be identical when they have the same elements, written: X=Y. This would be the case if, for instance, set X had the elements 1, 2, 3 and set Y also contained the elements 1, 2, 3. Sets can also be subsets of one another, if all the elements found in one are found in another, larger set. If set X has the elements 1, 2, 3, 4 and set Y has the elements 3, 4, then the set of elements 3, 4 is a subset of the sets X and Y. This is written as {3, 4} ⊆ {X, Y}. Here, it denotes that the set of elements 3, 4 is a subset of the set X and the set Y or that set X and set Y both contain elements 3 and 4. The use of the subset symbol is useful as we compile the sets that contain the specified coding categories of our interest.

For our defined sets A through L above, the following can be said:

- The union of sets A through L is:
  A ∪ L = {AU, AC, AD, ET, EC, EF, OA, OF, OE}
- The intersection of sets A through L is:
  A ∩ L = {OE}

In what follows, we investigate the sets, which include at least one code of OE and another code. We say "at least" one since there may be more than one code per document for OE, however as we explained in the previous paragraph, the frequency of the codes is not important here; only that the code is contained in the document (which are now referred to as individual sets). We use the union and intersection functions of set theory to analyze the coding categories that are included in sets that also include the code OE. Since we have just separated the sets that include the code OE, we can further analyze them. We systematically connect each different coding category with the code OE by first finding the proper subsets of the sets of policy documents. Then we perform the union and intersection functions to this group of sets.

- Sets that include elements OE and OA are {A, B, D, F, G, I, J}, that is:
  {OE, OA} ⊆ {A, B, D, F, G, I, J}
  Translated as the set OE and OA is a subsets of the sets A, B, D, F, G, I, J
- The union of the sets {A, B, D, F, G, I, J} is:
  {AU, AC, AD, ET, EC, EF, OA, OE} = {A ∪ B ∪ D ∪ F ∪ G ∪ I ∪ J}
  Translation as the set AU, AD, AC, ET, EC, EF, OA, OE is the union of the sets A, B, D, F, G, I, J

- The intersection of the sets {A, B, D, F, G, I, J} is:
  {AC, ET, OA, OE} = {A ∩ B ∩ D ∩ F ∩ G ∩ I ∩ J}
  Translation as the set AC, ET, OA, OE is the intersection of the sets A, B, D, F, G, I, J

- Sets that include elements OE and OF are {B, G, I, J}, that is:
  {OE, OF} ⊆ {B, G, I, J}
- The Union of the sets {B, G, I, J} is:
  {AU, AC, AD, ET, EC, EF, OA, OE, OF} = {B ∪ G ∪ I ∪ J}
- The Intersection of the sets {B, G, I, J} is:
  {AU, AC, AD, ET, EC, OA, OF, OE} = {B ∩ G ∩ I ∩ J}

- Sets that include elements OE and ET are {A, B, C, D, E, F, G, I, J, K, L}, that is:
  {OE, ET} ⊆ {A, B, C, D, E, F, G, I, J, K, L}
- The Union of the sets {A, B, C, D, E, F, G, I, J, K, L} is:
  {AU, AC, AD, ET, EC, EF, OA, OF, OE} = {A ∪ B ∪ C ∪ D ∪ E ∪ F ∪ G ∪ I ∪ J ∪ K ∪ L}
- The Intersection of the sets {A, B, C, D, E, F, G, I, J, K, L} is:
  {ET, OE} = {A ∩ B ∩ C ∩ D ∩ E ∩ F ∩ G ∩ I ∩ J ∩ K ∩ L}

- Sets that include elements OE and EC are {B, E, G, I, J, K, L}, that is:
  {OE, EC} ⊆ {B, E, G, I, J, K, L}
- The Union of the sets {B, E, G, I, J, K, L} is:
  {AU, AC, AD, ET, EC, EF, OA, OF, OE} = {B ∪ E ∪ G ∪ I ∪ J ∪ K ∪ L}
- The Intersection of the sets {B, E, G, I, J, K, L} is:
  {AU, AD, EC, OE} = {B ∩ E ∩ G ∩ I ∩ J ∩ K ∩ L}

- Sets that include elements OE and EF are {E, G, I}, that is:
  {OE, EF} ⊆ {E, G, I},
- The Union of the sets {E, G, I} is:
  {AU, AC, AD, ET, EC, EF, OA, OF, OE} = {E ∪ G ∪ I}
- The Intersection of the sets {E, G, I} is:
  {AU, AC, AD, ET, EC, EF, OE} = {E ∩ G ∩ I}

- Sets that include elements OE and AD are {A, B, E, G, I, J, K, L}, that is:
  {OE, AD} ⊆ {A, B, E, G, I, J, K, L},
- The Union of the sets {A, B, E, G, I, J, K, L} is:
  {AU, AC, AD, ET, EC, EF, OA, OF, OE} = {A ∪ B ∪ E ∪ G ∪ I ∪ J ∪ K ∪ L}
- The Intersection of the sets {A, B, E, G, I, J, K, L} is:
  {AD, ET, OE} = {A ∩ B ∩ E ∩ G ∩ I ∩ J ∩ K ∩ L}

- Sets that include elements OE and AC are {A, B, C, D, E, F, G, H, I, J, K}, that is:
  {OE, AC} ⊆ {A, B, C, D, E, F, G, H, I, J, K}
- The Union of the sets {A, B, C, D, E, F, G, H, I, J, K} is:
  {AU, AC, AD, ET, EC, EF, OA, OF, OE} = {A ∪ B ∪ C ∪ D ∪ E ∪ F ∪ G ∪ H ∪ I ∪ J ∪ K}
- The Intersection of the sets {A, B, C, D, E, F, G, H, I, J, K} is:
  {AC, OE} = {A ∩ B ∩ C ∩ D ∩ E ∩ F ∩ G ∩ H ∩ I ∩ J ∩ K}

- Sets that include elements OE and AU are {B, C, E, F, G, H, I, J, K, L}, that is:
  {OE, AU} ⊆ {B, C, E, F, G, H, I, J, K, L}
- The Union of the sets {B, C, E, F, G, H, I, J, K, L} is:
  AU, AC, AD, ET, EC, EF, OA, OF, OE} = {B ∪ C ∪ E ∪ F ∪ G ∪ H ∪ I ∪ J ∪ K ∪ L}
- The Intersection of the sets {B, C, E, F, G, H, I, J, K, L} is:
  {AU, OE} = {B ∩ C ∩ E ∩ F ∩ G ∩ H ∩ I ∩ J ∩ K ∩ L}

While all the above work has provided a rich description of how the coding elements have been structured with the documents, has it determined where the Badiouian void is? The key to investigating policy documents through a Badiouian lens is to understand what Badiou means by void, which for us is intrinsically tied with the event insofar as it is a necessary condition for the event to occur or be recognized by a subject. We understand Badiou's void as a place within a given situation in which something that is presentation is not representation, or when an element of a set in any given situation belongs but is not included. For our analysis here, the void could be the place in the policy discourses that we have collected and coded that depicts something that seems not to be intertwined with the main focus of the policy discussion. We have pinpointed the category of ontology and the subcategory of aesthetics as the anomaly in the discourse, since its code came up much more often than we had anticipated, and therefore it makes sense for us to investigate it further. Although the policy documents we have collected are a closed domain of policies in the United States that discuss STEM education, there is nevertheless more in them together than in any one document. This idea of the whole is greater than its parts is key to understanding the power of set theory to analyze policy. This is because set theory methodology allows for each document to remain faithful to its elements, while contributing to a larger discourse that is the domain or state of the situation of policies in the United States about STEM subjects, therefore creating a broader and more intricate body of analysis that can tell researchers more than studying each policy document alone or in tandem. The analysis we have undertaken above reveals the underlying reality of STEM policies in the United States from the perspective of a researcher who has believed and shown proof that ontological assumptions play a significant role in STEM education. Now, for the interpretation of the set theoretical operations we have performed.

First, when observing the union created by the above combination of sets, only one element does not occur in every set—that is, the OF—and it was missing in only one set when we grouped the elements OA and OE together. Next, we noticed that in most of the intersections of sets very few elements were included other than the ones we had controlled for. For example in the sets that had OE and AU, the only intersecting elements were OE and AU. This was not the case for a few intersecting sets however, for example, OE and EF, which had these elements in its intersection {AU, AC, AD, ET, EC, EF, OE} and OE and OF, which had {AU, AC, AD, ET, EC, OA, OF, OE}. Although the set that includes OF does not include EF and vice versa, the set that includes EF does not include OF. But it also does not include OA, but only OE. Yet, the set that includes OF does include OA, giving it one more element than its comparable here. Interestingly, when controlling for the sets with ontology of aesthetics and an epistemology of transformation or an ontology of fallibilism, there were many more elements that belonged. This may be a key finding since it seems it is within these two sets (OF and EF) that more elements belong, but those same elements are rarely represented in other more prominent sets. Perhaps even more fascinating is the fact that these same subcategories received the least amount of codes overall as indicated by the content analysis done in the preceding section of the chapter. Back to the union operation again, OF was found in all but one, which means that EF was in all of them. This means that EF was represented in all the policy documents that contained the element OE. EF was not present in any of the intersections sets, other than when it was controlled, yet when this was the case, the set that emerged from the intersection of this control contained almost all the elements, minus OF and OA, found in the entirety of the policy documents.

Thus, being the subject of this analysis of policy documents on STEM education, we claim that the void, at least for us, occurs within the discourse of a transformative epistemology. It is here that most of the other elements are included, yet the set itself (EF) is not included in the sets of its elements. Therefore, a fascinating turn in the Badiouian logic has occurred here. Rather than experiencing the event as the place where one element emerges from the void that either belongs but is not included or is presented but not represented, we have found instead a place where the very concept, which is not represented anywhere, included all the other concepts that are presented everywhere. The void occurs within the discourse of EF since this is the element least represented in the policy documents, yet on the rare occasions that it is, all other elements in all the policy documents are also represented.

Our findings here are perhaps different in degree but not in kind from Badiou's definition of the void. Badiou sees the void as occurring when some element in a set is presented but not represented; in other words, when something in a state of the situation belongs to it, but is not counted again or not allowed to be recognized for its belonging. In the policy set theoretical analysis carried out in this book, we find the void occurring in a different way. The element that was not represented in any of the sets is itself included in all the other sets. This translates for educational theoretic terms in interesting ways. How can the discourse that is not valued, which in this case is transformative pedagogy, contain the other more valued and normative discourses of the other categories, such as cognitive axiological objectives and absolutist ontological assumptions. These sets occurred in the policy documents that we coded and were not manipulated in any way. Thus, it seems that when policymakers do include the transformative epistemological stance, they also believe all other of the multiple axiological objectives, epistemological stances, and ontological assumptions are latent in it. These findings seem to contradict some of Badiou's assertion of revolutionary events and emerging truths, but we believe given the context of our analysis and theoretical frame, which is STEM education in the current political situation of the United States, such difference can be explained.

4
Critical Opportunities in STEM Education

Abstract: *This chapter is organized along the philosophical domains of ontology, epistemology, and axiology. Here, we consider the potential of STEM education in future educational theory and practice. We begin by exploring the possible contributions of critical theory in STEM education by attending to recent advancements in critical philosophies of mathematics, science, and technology; next with epistemology, we examine more deeply the transformative pedagogy of STEM education; and finally with axiology, we describe the values of STEM education that addresses the social and ecological crises.*

Keywords: aesthetics; ecojustice education; transformative pedagogy

Chesky, Nataly Z. and Mark R. Wolfmeyer. *Philosophy of STEM Education: A Critical Investigation.* New York: Palgrave Macmillan, 2015. DOI: 10.1057/9781137535467.0009.

Growing out of the previous chapters is this chapter's dedication to fully exploring the spaces where changes in the STEM discourse have the potential to occur. One such space is the aesthetic ontological appreciation of mathematics, which we contend is a transformative project in which such appreciation contextualizes liberation activities in the Marcusian sense. Second, in redefining what counts as science, ancient ways of knowing the biosphere reveal STEM's potentiality to address social and ecological crises. Similarly, redefining STEM's axiology, ontology, and epistemology of technology and engineering will move these content areas from their present circumstance as "the problem" to one in which they are "the solution." In all cases, we pick up right where the previous chapter leaves off, where our Badiouian exploration of STEM policies indicated a void of potentiality as epistemology transformative.

This chapter is organized along the philosophical domains we covered in Chapter 2: ontology, epistemology and axiology. This time, however, we discuss the what, how, and why of STEM education by including what some may consider alternative and we consider advanced philosophies. If STEM content is the space within which critical educators now have to work, it makes sense to confront the space directly with critical theories as they seem relevant. In what follows, we discuss "the what" of critical STEM education by attending to recent advancements in critical philosophies of mathematics, science, and technology; next with epistemology we examine more deeply the transformative pedagogy of STEM education; and finally with axiology we describe the values of a STEM education that addresses the social and ecological crises.

4.1 Post-modern conception of STEM subjects (Ontology)

In the previous chapters, we have cited several of the branches of philosophies of mathematics, science and technology to help in understanding the dominant narrative of the contents of STEM education. Here, we explore the relevant philosophies for what we hope the contents of STEM can become. As with other sections, we review some of the content areas as separated out into science, mathematics, and technology so as to paint a complete picture of possibilities for the STEM unit. Beginning with mathematics, we will look again at Alain Badiou's understanding of its role in social and political revolution and also at the recent turn in philosophy of mathematics education that points to the aesthetics of mathematics. As we discussed in Chapter 3, one of Badiou's most famous statements is that "mathematics is ontology," or more specifically, mathematics is the only discourse that can think ontologically (Badiou, 2005a). Mathematics has done more than simply provide an arena for abstract thinking or a language for gaining knowledge about our reality; it has been argued that our perception of mathematics frames our possible way of seeing the world, thereby excluding alternative conceptions of reality (Warnick and Stemhagen, 2007). Badiou writes that "Learning about mathematics, we come to also see ourselves as mathematical beings." (Fried, 2007, p. 219). Rarely do we stop and ask ourselves in what ways has our knowledge of mathematics structured our lives? This is an ontological question, since the way we perceive our life is directly related to language and societal norms that are constructed or are constantly being constructed that define and give meaning to us. Mathematics, being fundamental to our society, engulfs our perception of our world; it does this by framing how we understand economics, politics, religion, education, and ourselves, and even personal matters such as love and identity. For example, reflect upon to what extent our identities are structured around how much money we make, the size of clothes we wear, our credit score, and our income. In love matters, remember your first love and how it was compared on a continuum scale with previous lovers and imagined future ones or with quantitative speculation on how compatible two loves are in respect to their birthdays, incomes, and desired leisure activities. Even more to the point, numbers are not contested and are typically viewed as valuable important bits of knowledge. Mathematical language influences all aspects of our lives and therefore it is our contention that this language ought to be the utmost concern for educators and educational theorists, particularly ones that question the social injustices that are present in our society.

The axioms of mathematics allow Badiou to think about any given political or social situation in entirely new ways. But it is not just how mathematics thinks, but what or more specifically who is doing the thinking. Badiou's underlying assertion is that alternating our perception of what is a number can change our political and social organization in more democratic ways, and then it would be reasonable to evoke such a change in the education of mathematics itself. After all, it is within the discipline of mathematics that number is defined without critical reflection, and it is within the teaching and learning of mathematics that such concepts are propagated and not questioned. The critical theorists of critical mathematics pedagogy were right to claim that education of mathematics is the rightful place for higher consciousness to emerge, yet they did not dig deeply enough to wonder exactly how such changes may take place and from where they stem. The importance of mathematics as a pillar of our modern western paradigm presents ontological assumptions about what elements exist in our world and how they are structured. These premises are part of the hidden curriculum in mathematics and ought to be uncovered. By exposing how we are trained to perceive reality based on the way we learn mathematics, we can then seek alternatives within the discourse of mathematics itself. Thus, the past efforts in political pedagogies have failed to ignite real social change not because they were not worthy of such work or that such work was not extremely worthy in itself, but because they failed to see the underlying condition that necessitates the current inequalities that have characterized our society for so long.

What does this new notion of mathematics change about how we can think about mathematics education and the policies enacted to better it? "Badiou sees the role of mathematics as pivotal to a reversal of the excesses of postmodernity on the one hand and analytic philosophy on the other" (Peterson, p. 15 in den Heyer, 2009). Both poetry and mathematics are key possibilities for eventual sites. These eventual sites are Badiou's terms for particular times and places in history where newness can emerge, such as revolutions, a new movement in art or music, a new theory in science or mathematics, a new romantic love affair, and so on. Poetry is key for Badiou as an eventual site since it alters the way in which we understand and utilizes language, thereby opening a space for new awareness of ourselves and allowing our reality to emerge. Mathematics, on the other end of the truth conditions, can only name the space where the changes can occur. Thus, it does not so much as create these spaces, but the pivotal discourse for seeing it. Let us explain these truth conditions further.

For Badiou, there are four places for newness to occur (politics, science, love, and art). These truth events happen at a point at the edge of the void, which is defined as the space in which what is presented in a situation suddenly appears to some subject who becomes aware of its presence yet knows that this variable was never represented in a normal situation. In mathematics education, this void can be found in situations where we become aware of the ontological status of mathematics. According to Badiou, the void can only occur within particular contextual situations, which are always subjective in interpretation; yet, although they are universal in the sense that everyone can be privy to them, one cannot name the specific conditions by which such situations arise, nor can one generalize anything about them.

Aesthetics in mathematics, at least in the way we are utilizing it here, is about ontology; thus conceptualizing numbers and other mathematical entities as relationships is an ontological category that stands as an alternative to the absolutist and fallibilistic ontological perspective. Badiou in *The Handbook of Inaesthetics* (2005b) theorizes the connection between art, philosophy, and education. He writes, "the norm of art must be education, and the norm of education is philosophy" (p. 3). Further, "art itself that educates because it teachers of the power of infinity held within the tormented cohesion of a form" (ibid, p. 3). As Badiou explains, the link between art and philosophy is education; therefore it may be through education that aesthetics can be conceptualized in terms of mathematics. "Inaesthetic education aims to loosen the hold of sensibility on the minds of the populace, and ideally, to corrupt the youth" (Lehman, 2010, p. 177). Since both art and science are sites for truths to emerge, it is absolutely imperative for educators and philosophers to take notice. This might be especially true for mathematics since more and more art programs are being removed from the public school curriculum. While mathematics education cannot substitute for the aesthetic experiences students learn in a pure art class, it can however infuse art within its structure. Perhaps, as many have argued (Dehaene, 1997; Devlin, 2000; Sinclair, N., Pimm, D., Higginson, W. eds., 2006), this combination will help students learn high level mathematics more effectively.

What we must remember when thinking about philosophy of mathematics education is that philosophy, according to Badiou, does not produce any truths, however it "seizes truths and shows them, exposes them, announces that they exist" (2005a, p 14). As we move to the ontologies of science and technology in our hopeful alternative STEM sketch, this will again be a consistent theme. Essentially, critical educators can seize upon STEM as a space for contestations and constructions situated within social contexts.

In looking at philosophy of technology and science as a means to sketch the alternative STEM, we look to the advancements in philosophy of science that firmly root scientific ontologies in social contexts.

Here we will review in more detail the contributions of Paul Feyerabend, philosopher of science, and one social critic's views on technology. A quick glance at *Against Method* (1993) reveals several interesting points that Feyerabend makes. Scientific knowledge production is influenced by several factors, including politics, religion, and culture; scientific knowledge production is most fruitful when scientists are freed from rigid structures and hierarchy (anarchist science); and, in the following quote we clearly see Feyerabend's stance that scientific processes are but one way of obtaining knowledge:

> "It is thus possible to create a tradition that is held together by strict rules, and that is also successful to some extent. But is it desirable to support such a tradition to the exclusion of everything else? Should we transfer to it the sole rights for dealing in knowledge, so that any result that has been obtained by other methods is at once ruled out of court? And did scientists ever remain within the boundaries of the traditions they defined in this narrow way? These are the questions I intend to ask in the present essay. And to these questions my answer will be a firm and resounding NO." (p. 11)

For a critical, transformative STEM education, we suggest an ontology for science, like we did for mathematics, that embraces a nature of science where scientific knowledge production is *placed within* social life. The science education community, especially as scholars increasingly discuss science–technology–society and socioscientific issues, are beginning to adopt this philosophy. However, we suggest moving further beyond this nature of science as social construction; the STEM space can also reject western industrial culture's supreme faith in science. Science need not be regarded as the only way of solving problems, especially once we agree that scientific knowledge production is not entirely the result of rational, objective processes.

If the STEM space is to actively address the world's problems, such as the social and environmental crises, then it might be worth considering the prior relationship science and technology have had with said crises. Bowers (1993) suggests that conflating scientific and rational processes with technology coexists with the myth of progress that leads to ecologically disastrous consequences. In this way, we can think of an ontology for science-technology that is progress. This is understood to convey

> "the idea that certain changes are inevitable and good. Change is improvement. Modernity carries forward the assumption that change moves society forward and makes human society better off. [For example,] when we write

histories teaching that despite a few bad turns, things keep getting better every century." (Martusewicz, Edmundson, and Lupinacci, 2011, p. 72)

Bowers (1993) has found this cultural myth in science textbooks. He writes the textbook authors' efforts to make the connection

> "between scientific discoveries and the development of new technologies (computers, genetic engineering, telecommunications, etc.), further strengthened through use of appropriate visual images, further promotes the cultural myth that change is linear and progressive in nature."

Bowers locates the business of attending to "technological progress" by science textbooks as muddying the waters of philosophies of science and technology.

First off, as to be expected, science textbooks present the cultural myth of scientism/rationalism as discussed in Chapter 2. Most present "the authority of the scientific mode of thinking" (p. 136); if anything is mentioned of scientific doubts, it is casual, as one textbook quote demonstrates: "one peculiarity of the scientific method is that a hypothesis can never be formally proved but can only be disproved" (p. 138). Second, the authority of science is coupled with its relations to technological innovation. By associating the two, technology carries the authority and rationality put upon science.

Why is the cultural metaphor of progress, especially as it relates to technology, a myth, and, why does it lead to ecological and social crises? The answer to both questions is the same: technological innovation currently implies immediate implementation, with no basis for long term understanding of its consequences. As Bowers (1993) suggests, science textbooks do as good a job as any convincing readers of the myth, although "the myth is beginning to unravel as the media present incident after incident of the ecologically disruptive effects of technology (oil spills, toxic wastes, pollution, and so forth" (p. 139).

On a social level, technology also changes cultural and psychological processes in ways that are similarly not anticipated:

> The development and introduction into society of each new technology based on scientific knowledge also represents the initial stages of a cultural experiment. Changes within the culture that would result from the introduction of computers, for example, were not known at the time they were introduced into the work place and the classroom and proclaimed a great leap forward for humanity. We are just now beginning to recognize the unforeseen consequences of this technology in introducing new forms of dehumanization into

the work place and increasing surveillance of people's activities by employers and the state. (pp. 139–140)

When these catastrophes catch up with us, Bowers suggests that people

> "are likely to turn on the scientists and technologists with a vengeance that could be Biblical in scale. When the myth of progress ceases to be part of people's natural attitude, the claim that science can be viewed as separate from human concerns (and cultural beliefs) will be likely viewed as basically irresponsible and self-serving." (p. 141)

As with science textbooks, the very discourse of STEM education is quite guilty of proliferating the myth of progress. Associating science with technology, adding a dash of rational, objective, value-free mathematics, comes together as the perfect storm for progress. It is as if they say, "STEM will solve our problems, STEM has delivered us from past troubles, STEM will continue to do so." However, it is not difficult to point to STEM as the cause of our problems. Bowers discussion of the computer revolution brings to mind Microsoft's interest in STEM education.

The STEM space has the opportunity to challenge the assemblage of STEM and its associated myth of progress. By realizing the forces that created it, it can reject upfront the cultural myths of progress and rationalism outright. In recognizing the ontology of technology as divorced from the myth of progress, we can begin to imagine the axiology that the STEM space can embrace. In the axiology section of this chapter, we will return to Bowers and look carefully at E.F. Schumacher's "technology with a human face" as the underlying value for STEM education. In discussing future ontologies of mathematics, science, and technology here we see that the STEM unit's contents have the opportunity to play significant roles in social and environmental revolution.

4.2   Pedagogy of truths (Epistemology)

In this section, we sketch an idea of STEM teaching and learning that is grounded in the ontologies above and the axiology contained in the final section of this chapter. In other words, critical STEM that addresses the social and ecological crises resonates with the advanced philosophies of mathematics, science, and technology that we see as opportunities for the STEM unit. This original example of STEM teaching and learning draws upon the work of ethnomathematics. The example begins with a mathematical practice but, as shall be shown, this example is more correctly a STEM practice that folds in the other disciplines. We begin to imagine mathematics as a holistic inclusive discipline, one that has been historically and culturally intertwined with all human activities as well as inherently part of how humans come to make sense and interact with the ecological world. However, mathematics ought not only be utilized as a tool in which to uncover ecological crisis or explain how sustainable ecosystems may operate within a particular geological and cultural diverse system. As we discovered in the previous section, ontological questions about the nature of mathematics will continue to muddle the philosophical waters that separate positivist claims about numbers from fallibilistic ones.

The activity invites learners to experience a cultural practice of India which not only is rich in mathematical content, but also steeped in ecological significance. A Kolam is a "geometric drawing [that] adorns the ground at the entrance of even the humblest of homes in South India, creating an aesthetic local social space" (Thirumurthy and Simic-Muller, 2012; cited by Laine, 2009). A Kolam is composed of curved loops drawn around a grid of pattern of dots, called *pulli*. Kolams are said to have originated in 2500 BC in the Indus Valley civilization and are believed to bring wealth, happiness, and prosperity to the inhabitants of the dwelling. Women draw Kolams at the front entrance of their dwellings usually before or at dawn using colored rice powder. The powder welcomes birds, ants, and other small animals to eat it, thus "welcoming other beings into one's home and everyday life; a daily tribute to harmonious co-existence." (p. 1). Kolams have been theorized as an ethnomathematics activity (Thirumurthy and Simic-Muller, 2012), and Thirumurthy and Simic-Muller claim that "Kolam exposes children to historically accumulated and culturally developed bodies of knowledge and skills essential for household or individual functioning and well-being" (p. 310).

Rich in cultural significance, Kolam also provides deep mathematical learning about pattern recognition, algebraic reasoning, spatial sense, and geometric understanding. The authors of *Kolam: A Mathematical Treasure of South India* claim that the Kolam activity can be used to meet standards in algebraic reasoning as advocated by National Council of Teachers of Mathematics, 2000 (Thirumurthy and Simic-Muller, 2012). The geometric patterns for making Kolams are made by first creating a dot array or matrix. The array can be a rectangular or triangular shape or many variations of them. The dots can be equal or made in a horizontal sequence of consecutive odd or even numbers so that the first line has one dot, the second three, the third five, and so on, for example. Thus, unlike critiques of ethnomathematics, which claim that it does not provide rich mathematical experiences and weakens the agency for non-western children to engage with the dominant mathematics of the global world, the Kolam lesson can help every child, regardless of their cultural background, engage with an artistic, socially cultural meaningful activity that is also steeped in mathematics (Chenulu, 2007).

What we have just described is an ethnomathematics lesson, not an alternative STEM one. First, an ontological inquiry into the nature of the mathematical entities students were engaging with was not mentioned nor was the foundational assumptions about the relationship of mathematics objects, such as those dots and loops in the Kolam, brought into direct reflection. Second, the aesthetic nature of the activity itself, while mentioned as an art-based activity was simplified and not integrated holistically into the lesson. And last, the strong ecological significance of the Kolam was only initially revealed. We argue this to be at the center of the Kolam practice.

Thus, the Kolam thematic unit overlaps various traditional content areas: science (ecology), history, mathematics, and art. The mathematics and art aspects of the lesson can be experienced, while authentically coming back to the ecological and historical foundations established. Aesthetics plays a large role in this lesson since Kolams are indeed beautiful works of art made to commune with the sacred elements of life. Learners experience Kolams as creating art, an inherently aesthetic experience. They also become aware of the patterns that can be made by mathematical sequences and the relationship between each dot, or number of dots, to each other. In this sense, they experience pattern, relationship, spatial awareness, and beauty in mathematical ways, thus breaking the myth of the static abstract nature mathematics education typically gets packed as. Ontologically this has great significance as well. Teachers can explore the pattern of number sequences and how beautiful art pieces emerge from the connection of dots, or numbers. Deep philosophical questions can be unpacked about the nature of natural numbers and the unstable foundations of our Indio-Arabic number system. Learners can discuss the paradox of creating infinite patterns with finite resources, both at a high mathematical reasoning level with diagrams and computations, and at a high philosophical level through dialogue and logical argumentation.

Last, we believe it is important to decentralize topics for learners and create spaces in which one is uncomfortable, or uncertain of what one has learned or of what one believes is true. The Kolam lesson provides a perfect opportunity for this by reflecting upon one of the traditional purposes of making the Kolam at the front entrance of a dwelling using rice flour. That is to welcome living things into one's environment, to commune, and be encompassed by the ecological world around you. How is this practice diametrically opposed to modern homes? By using chemical cleaners and artificial building materials do not most western homes in fact attempt to achieve the opposite experience from traditional Indian homes—that of separation from the ecological world? But ants do find a way into wood, and mice like to come in from the cold, and spiders enjoy our ceilings and dark corners. Our battle against nature is unwinnable since we are indeed fighting against ourselves. The Kolam reminds us that the battle need not be foraged, that a harmonious relationship is possible and the world in which we live in is beautiful, complex, and in a state of ecological crisis. We feel this educational experience, based on our set theoretical findings in Chapter 3, has the potential to harness the revolutionary change Badiou has so reverently advocated for in education.

4.3 The axiological potential of alternative STEM education

The start of the 21st century, as a continued trend from the previous century, can be categorized as a time of rapid technological advances. While many of these advances may be signifiers of communities of healthier people and environments—for example, the development of medical technologies like the pace-maker; communication technologies like email, word processors, and the internet; or the development of alternate and clean energies like wind turbines or solar panels. However, these applications are less prominent than we might hope and more often against than in support of social justice and sustainability; technological advances have directly, or indirectly, accrued tremendous economic benefits for a small subsection of the world's population while contributing to a widening income gap inextricably tied to social suffering and environmental degradation (UNICEF, 2009).

At times the subsections of each chapter have privileged mathematics and science over technology. This was primarily because STEM education as it is currently talked about focuses more on mathematics and science than it does technology. However, when it comes to values, let us begin exploring the axiological possibilities (especially the critical ones) first with technology. If the STEM unit is to have any application as its value, and especially application for the world's crises, then technology seems a good place to start. Through E.F. Schumacher, we will see alternative values that could underpin technology in teaching STEM education. Resonating with Bowers' concerns over technological progress, Schumacher (1973) characterizes the technological crisis as follows:

> Suddenly, if not altogether surprisingly, the modern world, shaped by modern technology, finds itself involved in three crises simultaneously. First, human nature revolts against inhuman technological, organisational, and political patterns, which it experiences as suffocating and debilitating; second, the living environment which supports human life aches and groans and gives signs of partial breakdown; and third, it is clear to anyone fully knowledgeable in the subject matter that the inroads being made into the world's non-renewable resources, particularly those of fossil fuels, are such that serious bottlenecks and virtual exhaustion loom ahead in the quite foreseeable future. (p. 147)

In this way, technology has superseded its original definition and "acts like a foreign body" (p. 147). Schumacher calls for a return to technology's purpose. "The primary task of technology, it would seem, is to lighten the burden of work man [sic] has to carry in order to stay alive and develop his potential" (p. 148).

Part of Schumacher's vision considers the amount of time spent "engaging in real production," (p. 149) a phrase describing work that excludes all types of desk work and includes only the work related to what people need for survival. The ways technology has developed, so Schumacher argues, leads to a very minimal amount of engagement in real production, and this actually diminishes such engagement to practical nonexistence and a lack of social value attributed to it. As a consequence, "Modern technology has deprived man of the kind of work that he enjoys most, creative, useful work with hands and brains, and given him plenty of work of a fragmented kind, most of which he does not enjoy at all" (p. 151).

On the other hand, "technology with a human face," will embrace the knowledges coming from science and elsewhere to "lighten the burden of work" without eliminating our connections to work. Work satisfies the soul and should consume us, but not necessarily in the ways it did before we gained knowledges that can make this work equally, or more, satisfying. For example, gardening is a technology, lightening the burden of finding food as a hunger/gatherer might. Just as the gardener nurtures the plants' health and vitality, the technology of gardening nurtures the gardener. However in the technology of industrial farming, only the plants and animals are nurtured, and marginally at that. This technology has sliced the work of food growing into various disconnected segments, with workers not necessarily overseeing the entire project and much of the work being done by machines and chemicals.

For Schumacher, lightening the burden of work does not mean devaluing work and attempting to eliminate it. The sense of mainstream STEM education is the opposite, that in some ways science and technology will deliver us entirely from the burdens of work, perhaps even of the labor of living in our bodies. Scientist Ray Kurzweil has predicted that within 20 years, nanotechnologies will be capable of replacing all our vital organs and even reverse the aging process (Willis, 2009). This prediction, of course, could only be the case if science and technology continue to work hand-in-hand and are supported as they have been for the past 100 years. It would also require this "progress" remain unencumbered by significant obstacles, like an ecological catastrophe for instance.

Thus we suggest that technology in STEM education be a responsive activity in which scientific knowledges are applied to global environmental and social justice. Moving to mathematics, we recognize the role that this content area can play in such applications, and we will devote some space to that here. However, we also suggest that mathematics in STEM education need not be entirely for such purposes. In reviewing the ontologies and epistemologies of mathematics previously, we also suggest the ways that aesthetics of mathematics can be of value. In what follows we review a few key examples of such mathematics-focused STEM work.

Mathematics education projects sometimes suggest how we might challenge discourses of modernity as reviewed in Chapter 2. For example, de Freitas (2004, 2008) disentangles the binary of mathematics and the feminine and disrupts the gendered identities of mathematics discourse by critical reflexive narrative. Indeed, mathematics is still commonly attributed to masculine characteristics, such as cold, remote, hard, uncaring, rejecting, impersonal, empty, dead, fixed, and hierarchal.

de Freitas disrupts the narrative in the hope that her work "troubl[es] the power dynamic that structures the binary between the feminine and mathematics, while recognising the ways in which those same power relations produce the conditions of subjectivity" (2008, p. 289). Understanding that doing mathematics is an embodied experience, de Freitas and Sinclair (2013) proposed a practice that "goes further in proposing a new materialist ontology that seeks to study the mathematical body as an assemblage of human and non-human mathematical concepts" (p. 454). "They claimed that the body is an ecological system sustained through boundary negotiations, arguing that learning itself is an ecological process" (p. 454). They propose a "pedagogy of the concept" that animates concepts as both ontological and logical devices and draw on the philosopher of mathematics Gilles Châtelet in order to pursue this argument, elaborating on the way that "mathematical concepts partake of the mobility of the virtual, while learners, in engaging with this mobility, enter a material process of becoming." (p. 455). Sinclair and de Freitas work helps us disrupt the binaries of masculine/feminine gendered mathematics that are present in all forms of mathematics education, axiological, epistemological, and certainly, ontological. This work is a start, but there is still much more to be done.

A second example of an application of a critical mathematics: Skovsmose's (2011) reflection of the applications of mathematics lessons. Skovsmose discusses a particular mathematics project called "*A Terrible Small Number*" in which students examine the ecological and social implications of salmonella poisoning in Denmark (pp. 72–75). He asks educators to "consider to what extent an illusion of objectivity brings about a dissolution of responsibility." (p. 75). We can further ask how the mathematics and science used in Western culture is used and to whom it serves and oppresses.

Although there are other strands of critical approaches to education for social justice that are more mainstream (e.g., Wagner and Stinson, 2012), an underlying theme is that social injustices occur in many contexts worldwide and the act of teaching and learning mathematics and science ought to work towards becoming fully aware of human and ecological crises in order to establish ways in which agencies for change can occur. It is important to note that we are not advocating for mathematics education as a vehicle to address social justice issues in relation to ecological concerns. In other words, in many critical classrooms ecological concerns are seen as important but often as less important and separate from social justice. Such approaches reinforce a problematic value-hierarchized binary statement of culture/nature, which negates the interplay and interdependence between the two. The path that we point to is a STEM education that can support Gregory Bateson's (1972) "ecology of mind:" an ecological intelligence perhaps that might be thought of as a *less-than-rational* way of thinking. However, we not only find it to be an interesting educational project but also one inseparable from and not explicitly occurring in STEM education.

Mathematics and science need not be "useful" in all cases. The Kolam example from the previous epistemology section illustrates this. We suggest a return to the connectedness of mathematics and science, in which mathematical aesthetics is appreciated on their own terms and for nothing. It is our intention that such appreciation will further ground mathematics and science among the other cultural efforts, like art or music, rather than continue to elevate it to superior status. Thus, we reimagine the axiological objectives of STEM education to be centered around not only imagining sustainable technology, but also about harnessing aesthetic awareness, drawing on environmental-sensibilities, awakening cultural, gender, and class critical consciousness, and about nothing at all. Indeed, we hope that educators can engage in the act of teaching and learning mathematics and science to forget, if only for a moment, the mandated "student learning objectives" and allow the teaching act to be about the pure joy of experiencing the content together for no external purpose whatsoever.

5
Concluding Thoughts

Abstract: *In this short section, we argue for the full comprehension of STEM education policy so that its potential for critical education can be realized. This includes opening up the ontologies of STEM content areas in order to enact transformative education. We further draw on Badiouian analysis in describing the revolutionary potential of STEM education.*

Chesky, Nataly Z. and Mark R. Wolfmeyer . *Philosophy of STEM Education*: *A Critical Investigation*. New York: Palgrave Macmillan, 2015. DOI: 10.1057/9781137535467.0010.

As asserted elsewhere in this book, mathematical and science knowledge is ubiquitous in modern society; this fact leads us to conclude that it is precisely within such an all-encompassing discipline that revolutionary change has the greatest potential to emerge. The standardization and high stakes testing that have characterized policy reforms is not just about STEM content and how to teach it, but the content insofar as it is grounded on particular ontological orientations. Thus, if policy practices and ideologies can be questioned and viable alternatives can be made, then it can be due to a turn in the way we ontologically view the subject areas of STEM education.

Before alternatives can be envisioned and space for changes made, a strong comprehension of the policy discourse is necessary. Understanding of the situation is required, according to Badiou, for a subject to even have the possibility of being witness to a truth event. Since STEM is at the core of our knowledge as a society, it is vitally important for students to become fully knowledgeable about the core of its information, algorithms, processes, and methods. This statement may be disturbing for many learner-centered or social-constructivists educators since it does proclaim that a strong current western understanding of high-level mathematics and science is essential for every student. Nel Noddings wrote that not everyone needs algebra (Noddings, 2005). Other scholars have pointed to the exclusiveness and gentrification caused by mathematics education (e.g., Martin, 2008; Spillane, 2000). All these points are well founded, but the alternatives in STEM that follow from them are incomprehensible. Educators cannot chose to educate only a few "talented" students in STEM, nor should they spend precise school time teaching long forgotten algorithms for multiplication. We cannot simply ignore the situation as it is presented to us, nor can we hope to find a safe haven outside the state of the situation that cannot be influenced if not subsumed by the situation eventually. After all, we live in a modern western central world here in the U.S., where mathematics and science are embedded in most products that we use everyday. A strong comprehension of fractions cannot do any harm, but a misunderstanding of fractions can do massive amounts of harm, not only in the pursuit of finding gainful employment, and being a productive democratic citizen, but in the overall meta-cognitive understanding of one's life, self, and world around him. Similarly, a misunderstanding of scientific knowledge regarding human health can do significant harm.

Amarthya Sen's (2000) definition of human capital is "expansion of the capabilities of persons to lead the kind of lives they value and have reason to value" (p. 18). Reducing education to only serve workforce or economic demands lessens the way humankind has conceived of knowledge. Reducing learners or citizens to human capital, which are only necessary in terms of what capital they can produce for their nation, dehumanizes children and their families. It cheapens our values as a society and drastically reduces the possible social justice capabilities our education system can still, in our optimistic minds, create. On the other side, diluting education to erase the rigor and challenge in a discipline so highly influential to humankind would be a travesty. Luckily, the current national STEM education policies have not set out to do any of the above. In fact, the policies seem to have opened a small space for positive changes in STEM education to take place. Such changes have the potential to change our societal norms about STEM subjects, and the way it shapes our lives, for the better.

The set theoretical analysis done at the end of Chapter 3 generated interesting and surprising findings. Connecting an aesthetic ontological view of STEM with a transformative epistemology seems to be where a Badiouian event has the potential to emerge. To review, epistemological category believes knowledge is equal to power and that teaching this axiom in STEM education is crucial for developing the critical consciousness Freire and others critical theorists have strived for. The words that we found in policy documents that relate to this code are transformative, critical, awareness, power, and empower. An example from one of the documents for this code is "Mathematics empowers us to better understand the information world in which we live" (*Everybody Counts*). However, it is not clear if the way in which the word "empowers" relates to the way transformative epistemologies might envision it. Perhaps, this is not the point, especially in relation to policy documents, which are written in a more or less rhetorical format.

Given the research questions that grounded this book, we cannot offer further analysis on the link between transformative epistemology and a Badiouian event. However, what we can offer based on the findings generated from the set theoretical method we incorporated are the conditions by which an event might occur, or where Badiou's void might be found. Based on our analysis of the "state of the situation," we must say that the void is located in transformative epistemologies that take into account all the interrelationships in the complex discourse of STEM education policy reforms. Thus, it is not that transformative epistemologies can themselves elicit the events that have the potential to create subjects and radically change our society for the better; rather, it is the entanglement of an aesthetic ontological view of STEM content with a subtle understanding of its historical and philosophical connection with the absolutist and fallibilist view. All this must be coupled with an expert understanding of all the axiological claims made in policy discourses. According to our analysis, transformative epistemology, once it gets filtered through an ontological aesthetic way of understanding mathematics and science, has the potential to ignite an event, and thus to create a Badiouian subject; whether this subject is a mathematics/science teacher, a mathematics/science learner, or an educational researcher only makes a difference in the way he/she interprets and chooses to act once experiencing such an "event." As Badiou himself confesses, a subject must always "wager" or "... decide upon the undecidable" (2000). In *Ethics* (2000), Badiou theorizes a new type of universal ethics, one based on a subject remaining faithful to the truth event he/she has witnessed. Barbour (2010) writes: "For Badiou, everything 'hinges on the possibility that some subject will encounter or experience some truth or experience some event and on the basis of that encounter or experience, be utterly compelled to decide a new way of being and 'invent a new way of acting in situation'" (cited Badiou 2001, pp. 41–42).

Hannah Arendt (1958) once explained, "to be political is to be in a polis, meaning that everything is decided through words and persuasion and not through force and violence." Educational policy is indeed about words and their meaning, rhetoric and its level of persuasion. It is the work of educational theorists and researchers to always keep a watchful eye on political decisions as they relate to education, to question their coherence, to ask critical questions about their underlying objectives, and to seek more equitable solutions to their consequences.

Revolution, for us, is not an antagonistic warfare but a subtle introspective creative process that although happens under the situation as it stands, slowly but surely erupts to change society completely. It is our knowledgeable conviction that once we begin to view the world as a collection of beautifully woven patterns or structures and gain the knowledge that grants us, as a distinct being that is never simply a binary collection of cells, the power to feel not only an integral part of such a world, but as an agent in transforming it, real lasting revolutionary change will take place. But before that happens, we are content to continue working in the field of higher education, educating future mathematics and science teachers who will be on the front lines of educational policy decisions and implementation. Perhaps, it is here that the kind of subject Badiou prophesied about is most needed and where revolutionary thoughts can best flourish.

References

Apple, M. (1992). Do the standards go far enough? Power, policy, and practice in mathematics education. *Journal for Research in Mathematics Education.* 23(5), 412–431.

Apple, M. (2003). Competition, knowledge, and the loss of educational vision. *Philosophy of Music Education Review.* 11(1), 3–23.

Arendt, H. (1958). *The Human Condition.* Chicago: University of Chicago Press.

Atweh, B. (2007). *Pedagogy for Socially Response-able Mathematics Education.* Paper presented at the Australian Association of Research in Education, Fremantle, West Australia.

Badiou, A. (2006). Philosophy as creative repetition. *The Symptom Online Journal for Lacan.com.* http://www.lacan.com/symptom8_articles/badiou18.html (2 of 6) 2/24/07

Badiou, A. (2008). *Number and Numbers.* Malden, MA: Polity.

Badiou, A. & Feltham, O. Trans. and Ed. (2003). *Infinite Thought: Truth and the Return of Philosophy.* New York. Continuum.

Badiou, A. & Hallward, P. Trans. (2003). *Ethics: An Essay on the Understanding of Evil.* New York: Verso.

Badiou, A. & Feltham, O. Trans. (2005a). *Being and Event.* New York: Continuum.

Badiou, A. & Toscano, A. Trans. (2005b). *Handbook of Inaesthetics.* California: Standford University Press.

Barbour, C. (2010). Militants of truth, communities of equality: Badiou and the ignorant schoolmaster. *Educational Philosophy and Theory.* 42(2), 251–262.

Bateson, G. (1972). *Steps to an Ecology of Mind.* Chicago: University of Chicago Press.

Berry, R. & Ellis, M. (2005). The paradigm shift in mathematics education: Explanations and implications of reforming conceptions of teaching and learning. *The Mathematics Educator.* 15(1), 7–17.

Biesta, G. (2010). Witnessing deconstruction in education: Why quasi-transcendentalism matters. In C. Reutenberg (Ed.), *What Do Philosophers of Education Do? (And How Do They Do It?)* (pp. 74–86). London: Blackwell.

Blades, D. (2006). Levinas and an ethics for science education. *Educational Philosophy & Theory.* 38(5), 647–664.

Blenkinsop, S. Ed. 2009. *The Imagination in Education: Extending the Boundaries of Theory and Practice.* Tyne, UK: Cambridge Scholars Publishing.

Bosse, M. (2006). Beautiful mathematics and beautiful instruction: Aesthetics within the NCTM standards. *International Journal for Mathematics Teaching and Learning.* 28, 172–243.

Bowers, C. (1993). *Education, Cultural Myths, and the Ecological Crises: Toward Deep Changes.* Albany, NY: State University of New York Press.

Brantlinger, A. (2011a). Rethinking critical mathematics: A comparative analysis of critical, reform, and traditional geometry instructional texts. *Education Studies in Mathematics.* 78(3), 395–411.

Brantlinger, A. (2011b). A view from the other side: Partitioner research on critical mathematics pedagogy in an urban high school. In K. A. Scott & W. J. Blanchett (Eds.), *Urban Education Settings: Lessons Learned and Implications for Future Practice.* Charlotte, NC: Information Age Publishing.

Breiner, J. et al. (2012). What is STEM? A discussion of conceptions of STEM in education and partnerships. *School Science and Mathematics.* 112(1), 3–11.

Bridges, D. & Smith, R. (2007). *Philosophy, Methodology, and Educational Research.* Malden, MA: Blackwell Publishing.

Brown, R. et al. (2011). Understanding STEM: Current perceptions. *Technology and Engineering Teacher.* 70(6), 5–9.

Brown, T. (2010). Truth and the renewal of knowledge: The case of mathematics education. *Educational Studies in Mathematics.* 75, 329–343.

Burbaker, A. (2008). Metaphysics and method: Mathematics and the two canons of theory. *New Literary History.* 30(4), 869–890.

Burgh, G. & Nichols, K. (2012). The parallels between philosophical inquiry and scientific inquiry: Implications for science education. *Educational Philosophy & Theory.* 44(10), 1045–1059.

Burbules, N. & Linn, M. (1991). Science education and philosophy of science: Congruence or contradiction? *International Journal of Science Education.* 13(3), 227–241.

Bybee, R. (2010). Advancing STEM education: A 2020 vision. *Technology and Engineering Teacher.* 70(1), 30–35.

Campos, D. (2010). Peirce's philosophy of mathematics education: Fostering reasoning abilities for mathematical inquiry. *Studies in Philosophical Education.* 29, 421–439.

Charalabous, C. & Philloppou, G. (2010). Teachers' concerns and efficacy beliefs about implementing a mathematics curriculum reform: Integrating two lines of inquiry. *Educational Studies in Mathematics.* 75(1), 1–21.

Chenulu, S. (2007). Teaching mathematics through the art of Kolam. *Mathematics Teaching in the Middle School.* 12(8), 422–428.

Clemens, J. (2001). Platonic meditations: The work of Alain Badiou. *Pii.* 11, 200–229.

Cobb et al. (1992). A constructivist alternative to the representational view of mind in mathematics education. *Journal of Research in Mathematics Education.* 23(1), 2–33.

Crannell, A. (2009). Mathematics and the aesthetic: A book review. *Notices of the AMS.* 56(2), 233–236.

Cross, C. (2004). *Political Education: National Policy Comes of Age.* New York: Teachers College Press.

D'Ambrosio, U. (2001). Mathematics and peace: A reflection on the basic of western civilization. *Leonardo.* 34(4), 327–332.

Davis, P. & Hersh, R. (1980). *The Mathematical Experience.* Brighton, England: Harvester.

Davison, D., Mitchell, J., & Montana, B. (2008). How is mathematics education philosophy reflected in the wars. *The Montana Mathematics Enthusiast.* 5(1), 143–154.

Davydov, V. (1995). The influence of L. S. Vygotsky on education theory, research, and practice. *Educational Researcher.* 24(3), 12–21.

de Freitas, E. (2004). Plotting intersections along the political axis: The interior voice of dissenting mathematics teachers. *Educational Studies in Mathematics.* 55(1), 259–274.

de Freitas, E. (2008). Mathematics and its other: (Dis)locating the feminine. *Gender and Education.* 20(3), 281–290.

de Freitas, E. & Sinclair, N. (2013). New materialist ontologies in mathematics education: The body in/of mathematics. *Educational Studies in Mathematics.* 83, 453–470.

Dehaene, S. (1997). *The Number Sense: How the Mind Creates Mathematics.* New York, NY: Oxford University Press.

den Heyer, K. (2009). Education as an affirmative invention: Alain Badiou and the purpose of teaching and curriculum. *Educational Theory.* 59(4), 442–463.

Dejarnette, N. K. (2012). America's children: Providing early exposure to STEM (Science, Technology, Engineering, and Math) initiatives. *Education.* 133(1), 77–84.

Descartes, R. (1637). Discourse on method of rightly conducting one's reason and of seeking truth in the sciences. Leiden, The Netherlands.

Devlin, K. (2000). *The Math Gene: How Mathematical Thinking Evolved and Why Numbers Are Like Gossip.* New York: Basic Books.

Eglash, R. (2002). *African Fractal: Modern Computing and Indigenous Design.* New Brunswick, NJ: Rutgers University Press.

Ernest, P. Ed. (1994). *Mathematics, Education and Philosophy: An International Perspective.* Bristol, PA: The Falmer Press.

Ernest, P. (2004). What is the philosophy of mathematics education. *Contribution for Discussion Group 4.*

Feyerabend, P. (1978, 1982). *Science in a Free Society.* London: New Left Books.

Feyerabend, P. (1987). *Farewell to Reason.* London, New York: Verso.

Feyerabend, P. (1993). *Against Method 3rd edition.* London, New York: Verso.

Frankenstein, M. (1983). Critical mathematics education: An application of Paulo Preire's epistemology. *Journal of Education.* 165(4), 315–338.

Fried, M. (2007). Didactics and history of mathematics: Knowledge and self-knowledge. *Educational Studies in Mathematics.* 66, 203–223.

Gabbard, D. (2000). *Knowledge and Power in the Global Economy: Politics and the Rhetoric of School Reform.* Mahwah, NJ: Lawrence Erlbaum Associates.

George, et al. (2001). *In Pursuit of a Diverse Science, Technology, Engineering, and Mathematics Workforce.* Recommended Research Priorities to Enhance Participation by Underrepresented Minorities. American Association for the Advancement of Science. Washington

D.C. National Science Foundation. American Association for the Advancement of Science.

Greer, B. & Mukhopadhyay, S. (2003). What is mathematics education for? *Mathematics Educator.* 13(2), 2–6.

Gutstein, E. (2006). *Reading and Writing the World with Mathematics: Towards a Pedagogy for Social Justice.* New York, NY: Routledge.

Gutstein, E. (2008). The political context of the national mathematics advisory panel. *The Montana Mathematics Enthusiast.* 6(2&3), 415–422.

Hallward, P. Ed. (2006). *Think Again: Alain Badiou and the Future of Philosophy.* New York, NY: Continuum Studies in Philosophy.

Hersh, R. (1993). Proving is convincing and explaining. *Educational Studies in Mathematics.* 24(4), 389–399.

Hodson, D. (2004). Time for action: Science education for an alternative future. *International Journal of Science Education.* 25(6), 645–670.

Holma, K. (2010). The strict analysis and the open discussion. In C. Reutenberg (Ed.), *What Do Philosophers of Education Do? (And How Do They Do It?).* London: Blackwell Publishers.

Honig, M. Ed. (2006). *New Directions in Education Policy Implementation.* Albany, NY: State University of New York Press.

Irzig, G. (2000). "Back to basics": A philosophical critique on constructivism. *Science and Education.* 9(6), 621–639.

Jackmore, J. & Lander, H. (2005). Researching policy. In B. Somekhi & L. Lewin (Eds.). *Research Methods in the Social Sciences* (pp. 97–104). London, Enlgan: Sage Publishers.

Katz, J. (1995). What mathematical knowledge could be. *Mind.* 104(415), 481–522.

Kelly. A. (2008). Reflections on the national mathematics advisory panel final report. *Educational Researcher.* 37(9), 561–564.

Kilpatrick, J. (2001). Understanding mathematical literacy: The contribution of research. *Educational Studies in Mathematics.* 47(1), 101–116.

Kilpatrick, J., Quinn, H., & National Academy of Education (2009). Science and mathematics education. Education Policy White Paper.

Krippendorff. K. (2004). *Content Analysis: An Introduction to Its Methodology.* Thousand Oaks: Sage Publications.

Kubli, F. (2010). Do we need a philosophy of science education? *Interchange.* 41(4), 315–321.

Kuhn, T. (1962). *The Structure of Scientific Revolutions.* Chicago: University of Chicago Press.

Kumar, D., & Chubin, D. (2000). *Science, Technology and Society: A Sourcebook on Research and Practice.* Dordrecht: Kluwer.

Lakatos, I. (1976). *Proofs and Refutations.* Cambridge: Cambridge University Press.

Laughter, J. & Adams, A. (2012). Culturally relevant science teaching in middle school. *Urban Education.* 47, 556–561.

Lehman, R. (2010). Between the science of the sensible and the philosophy of art: Finitude in Alain Badiou's inaesthetics. *Journal of Theoretical Humanities.* 15(2), 171–184.

Lester, F. (2005). On the theoretical, conceptual, and philosophical foundations for research in mathematics education. *ZDM.* 37(6), 457–467.

Lewis, T. & Cho, D. (2005). Education and event: Thinking radical pedagogy in the era of standardization. *Studies in Media & Information.* 5(2), 1–11.

Lloyd, G. (1995). *The Man of Reason: The "Male" & "Female" in Western Philosophy.* London: Routledge.

Marshall, C. & Rossman, G. (1999). *Designing Qualitative Research.* Newsbury Park: Sage Publications.

Martin, D. (2003). Hidden assumptions and unaddressed questions in mathematics or all rhetoric. *The Mathematics Educator.* 13(2), 7–21.

Martin, D. (2008). E(race)ing race from a national conversation on mathematics teaching and learning: The national mathematics advisory panel as white institutional space. *The Montana Mathematics Enthusiast.* 15(2&3), 387–398.

Martusewicz, R., Edmundson, J., & Lupinacci, J. (2011). *EcoJustice Education: Toward Diverse, Democratic and Sustainable Communities.* New York, NY: Routledge.

National Science Teachers Association. (NSTA). (2004). Scientific inquiry http://www.nsta.org/about/positions/inquiry.aspx

Niaz, M. (2004). Inquiry learning: A Venezuelan perspective. In Abd-El Khalick, F. et al. (Eds.), *Inquiry in Science Education: International Perspectives.* Wiley Periodicals, Inc. 406–407.

Noddings, N. (2005). *The Challenge to Care in Schools: An Alternative Approach to Education.* New York: Teachers College, Columbia University.

Ozga, J. (2004). *Policy Research in Educational Settings: Contested Terrain.* Philadelphia, PA: Open University Press.

Perakyla, A. (2005). Analyzing talk and text. In N. K. Denzin & Y. Lincoln (Eds.), *The Sage Handbook of Qualitative Research*, 3rd edition (pp. 869–886). Thousand Oaks, CA: Sage.

Phillips, D. (2007). The contested nature of empirical educational research (and why philosophy of education offers little help). In D. S. Bridges, R. (Ed.), *Philosophy, Methodology, and Educational Research* (pp. 311–331). Malden, MA: Blackwell.

Pierce, C. (2012). The promissory future(s) of education: Rethinking scientific literacy in the era of biocapitalism. *Educational Philosophy & Theory*. 44(7), 721–745.

Popkewitz, T. (2004). The alchemy of the mathematics curriculum: Inscriptions and the fabrication of the child. *American Education Research Journal*. 41(1), 3–34.

Postman, N. (1995). *The end of education*. New York, NY: Vintage Books.

Radford, L. (2006). The anthropology of meaning. *Educational Studies in Mathematics*. 61(1&2), 39–65.

Resnik, M. (1981). Mathematics as a science of patterns: Ontology and reference. *Nous*. 15(4), 529–550.

Restivo, S. Bendegam, J., & Fischer, R. Eds. (1993). *Math Worlds: Philosophical and Social Studies of Mathematics and Mathematics Education*. Albany, NY: State University Press.

Reys, R. (2001). Curricular controversy in the math wars: A battle without winners. *The Phi Delta Kappan*. 83(3), 255–258.

Roth, W. and Barton A. (2004). *Rethinking Scientific Literacy*. New York: Routledge.

Rowlands, S. and Carson, R. (2001). The contradictions in the constructivist discourse. *Philosophy of Mathematics Education Journal* (P. Ernest, Ed.) No. 14 (May 2001).

Sanders, M. (2009). STEM, STEM education, STEM mania. *Technology Teacher*. 68(4), 20–26.

Schoenfeld, A. (2004). The math wars. *Educational Policy*. 18(1), 253–286.

Schmidt, W. (2012). At the precipice: The store of mathematics education in the United States. *Peabody Journal of Education*. 87(1), 133–156.

Schmidt, W., Houand, R., & Cogan, L. (2001). A coherent curriculum: The case of mathematics. *American Educator*. Summer 2002, 1–18.

Schmidt, W., Wang, H., & McKnight, C. (2005). Curriculum coherence: An examination of U.S. Mathematics and science content standards from an international perspectives. *Journal of Curriculum Studies.* 37(5), 525–559.

Schumacher, E. (1973). *Small is Beautiful: Economics As If People Mattered.* New York, NY: Harper & row.

Sen, A. (2000). *Development as Freedom.* New York, NY: Alred A. Knopf.

Shapiro, S. (1997). *Philoophy of Mathematics: Structure and Ontology.* New York, NY: Oxford Universit Press.

Sharp, L. & Richardson, T. (2001). Reflections on Foucauldian discourse analysis in planning and environmental policy research. *Journal of Environmental Policy & Planning.* 3(3), 193–209.

Sinclair, N. (2001). The aesthetic *is* relevant. *For the Learning of Mathematics.* 21(1), 25–32.

Sinclair, N., Pimm, D., & Higginson, W. Eds. (2006). *Mathematics and the Aesthetic.* New York, NY: Springer.

Skovsmose, O. (1994). *Towards a Philosophy of Critical Mathematics Education.* Boston, MA: Kluwer Academic Publishers.

Skovsmose, O. (2006). Research, practice, uncertainty and responsibility. *Journal of Mathematical Behavior.* 35(4), 267–284.

Spillane, J. (2000). Cognition and policy implementation: District policymakers and the reform of mathematics education. *Cognition and Instruction.* 18(2), 141–179.

Spring, J. (2010). *The American School: From the Puritans to No Child Left Behind.* New York, NY: McGraw-Hill.

Sriraman, B. & English, L. (2010). Surveying theories and philosophies of mathematics education. In *Advances in Mathematics Education: Theories of Mathematics Education: Seeking New Frontiers* (pp. 7–32). Berlin Heiderberg: Springer.

Steiner, H. (1987). Philosophical and epistemological aspects of mathematics and their interaction with theory and practice in mathematics education. *For the Learning of Mathematics.* 7(1), 7–13.

Stigler, J. & Hiebert, J. (2004). Improving mathematics teaching. *Educational Leadership.* 61(5), 12–17.

Stone, D. (2002). *Policy Paradox: The Art of Political Decision Making.* New York, NY: Norton & Company.

Thirumurthy, V. & Simic-Muller, K. (2012). Kolam: A mathematical treasure of South India. *Childhood Education.* 80(5), 309–314.

Thom, R. (1973). Modern mathematics: Does it exist? In A. G. Howson (Ed.), *Developments in Mathematical Education* (pp. 195–209). Cambridge, MA: Cambridge University Press.

Topcu et al. (2014). Socioscientific issues in science education: The case of Turkey. *Educational Sciences: Theory & Practice.* 14(6), 2340–2348.

Tucker, M. (2012). STEM: Why it makes no sense. National Center on Education and the Economy. http://www.ncee.org/2012/06/stem-why-it-makes-no-sense/

Tymoczko, T. (1993). Value judgments in mathematics: Can we treat mathematics as an art? In A. White (Ed.), *Essays in Humanistic Mathematics* (pp. 57–78). Washington, D.C.: Mathematical Association of America.

UNICEF (2009). The state of the world's children: Special edition. UNICEF. Retrieved on January 25, 2014 from http://www.unicef.org/rightsite/sowc/pdfs/SOWC_Spec Ed_CRC_Main Report_EN_090409.pdf

Valero, P. (2004). Socio-political perspectives on mathematics education. *Mathematics Education Library.* 35, 5–23.

von Glasersfeld, E. (1991). *Radical Constructivism in Mathematics Education.* Dordrecht: Kluwer.

Wager, A. & Stinson, D. Eds. (2012). *Teaching Mathematics for Social Justice: Conversations with Educators.* Reston, VA: National Council of Teachers of Mathematics.

Wang, H. (2001). Aesthetic experience, the unexpected, and curriculum. *Journal of Curriculum and Supervision.* 17(1), 90–94.

Warnick, B. & Stemhagen, K. (2007). Mathematics teachers as moral educators: The implications of conceiving of mathematics as a technology. *Journal of Curriculum Studies.* 39(3), 303–316.

Wigner, E. (1960). The unreasonable effectiveness of mathematics in natural science. *Communications on Pure and Applied Mathematics.* 13(1). 1–14.

Willis, A. (2009). Immortality only 20 years away says scientist. *The Telegraph.* Available at http://www.telegraph.co.uk/news/science/science-news/6217676/Immortality-only-20-years-away-says-scientist.html

Wolfmeyer, M. (2014). *Math Education for America? Policy Networks, Big Business, and Pedagogy Wars.* New York, NY: Routledge.

Zeidler et al. (2005). Beyond STS: A research-based framework for socioscientific issues education. Published online at Wiley InterScience (www.interscience.wiley.com).

Index

absolutist, 21
aesthetic, 21
Arendt, Hannah, 93

Back to Basics Act, 39
Badiou, Alain, 45
Bateson, Gregory, 89
biocapitalism, 40, 41
biopower, 41
Bowers, 82

Châtelet, Gilles, 88
citizen science, 41
constructivism, 20
constructivist pedagogies, 27
content analysis, 52, 53
critical mathematics pedagogy, 32, 34

Descartes, Rene, 24

Eglash, Ron, 33
Ernest, Paul, 13, 38
ethnomathematics, 32

fallibilist, 21
Feyerabend, Paul, 24, 31, 80
Fibonacci, 30
Foucault, Michel, 11, 41
Freire, Paulo, 34

Galileo, 48
Godel, 22
Gutstein, Eric, 40

human capital, 36
human capital development, 11

Kolam, 83
Krippendorff, Klaus, 54
Kuhn, Thomas, 24, 25

Marcuse, Herbert, 76

A Nation at Risk, 5
National Academy of Education, 7
National Center on Education and the Economy, 5
National Council of Teachers of Mathematics (NCTM), 10, 22, 27
National Defense Education Act, 5
National Science Foundation, 3, 5, 7
National Science Teachers Association (NSTA), 30
natures of science, 20
NCTM, 6
New Math, 39
No Child Left Behind Act, 39
Noddings, Nel, 91

pedagogy of the concept, 88
Piaget, Jean, 27, 28
Poincare, 22
Postman, Neil, 42
President Eisenhower, 5

radical constructivism, 29
radical constructivists, 27
Resnik, Michael, 22, 48

Schumacher, E.F., 86
science-technology-society (STS), 14
Sen, Amarthya, 92
set theory, 45
Shapiro, Stewart, 22, 48
situation, 62, 63
  singular situation, 63
Skovsmose, Ole, 13, 34, 88
social constructivists, 27
socio-scientific issues (SSI), 14, 26, 36

socioscientific issues, 80
Sputnik, 5
STEM pipeline, 9

transformative pedagogies, 32, 35
truth event, 47, 49, 61, 78

UNICEF, 85

void, 47, 49, 63, 64, 69, 78
Vygotsky, Lev, 27, 28

Wigner, Eugene, 21, 28
Wittgenstein, Ludwig, 29

CPSIA information can be obtained
at www.ICGtesting.com
Printed in the USA
LVOW12*0748210218
567388LV00010B/189/P

9 781137 535450